THE GARBAGE MURDERS

FRANK SANTORSOLA

Greg & Kelli,

Enjoy.

Uncle Frankie

BAXTER

Frank Santorsola

Baxter Productions Inc.
308 Main St
New Rochelle NY 10801
www.baxterproductionsmedia.com

This book is a work of fiction. The names, characters, businesses, places, events and incidents are
either the products of the author's imagination or used in a fictitious manner. Any resemblance to
actual persons, living or dead, or actual events is purely coincidental.

ISBN 978-0-9982773-0-1

First Edition
First Printing

THE GARBAGE MURDERS

FRANK SANTORSOLA

Dedication

This book is dedicated to my lovely wife and
literary consultant Christina.
It seems that our journey together never ceases
to amaze me.

FORWARD

The life of a law enforcement officer is something most people think they understand. They nod with faint appreciation about the good job that is performed, and stand at the ready to criticize when one of us steps out of line. We are more than the necessary evil we are made out to be, but are appreciated only when we are needed. Let's face it, the only real contact most of us have with law enforcement is when something adversarial happens in your life. From the red light you never ran through because it was yellow, to the time when the ugliest person in the world stole your worldly possessions. The amount of interactions a police officer has in a day with the public can be overwhelming. Chances are I already saw death, a robbery victim, and a really bad accident before I had lunch and then came to you to handle the blocked driveway you are furious over. And you wonder why I am not more congenial.

That is the life of a cop. The pressures that come with the job are immense. It is what you sign on for and what you learn to deal with. If you don't, you internally explode. And then there comes a person like Frank Santorsola.

Within the "Blue Walls of Silence" there is a real appreciation for the officers who go undercover to assume an identity not their own, who forgo the traditional expectations of performance and operate in a world where perception becomes reality. Some might say it is a calling, based on the sacrifices asked of the officers who volunteer for these roles. A level of sacrifice we can never understand, nor are most willing to make. Think about it, as an officer, you realize and understand that at any given moment in your career, your life can be sacrificed for someone you probably don't know. You accept this challenge and are eager to perform. But the role of a true undercover is so much more involved than that.

The emotional, physical and mental toll is something we can never really appreciate or fully grasp. The loss of family, the loneliness and deafening silence can be unbearable to the average man. The dedication to service is tested not just for the daily tour of duty, but for years to come long after retirement. Why they do it is a personal choice. But whatever the reason, it always comes down to a belief in a principle they are willing to fight for regardless of the personal cost. Dying would be an easy out. In their world, death is a slow process of a million small cuts.

The general public may never know or understand the hows and whys of what makes an undercover tick. This book offers a peek into their world. As a former law enforcement officer who had the privilege to meet, and work with some of the best undercover's in the world, I can simply say the world is a better place because of people like Frank Santorsola.

Once you read this book, you will understand why.

Sal Lifrieri
Detective, 1st Grade
NYPD (retired)

PREFACE

The following story, "Miranda Writes / The Garbage Murders" is fact - based fiction, and a sequel to my first book, "Miranda Writes / Honor and Justice". It's my account of the events that occurred while I was assigned to investigate a number of organized crime related murders in the private sanitation business and the other illegal activities in which they were involved. Working deep undercover for the Westchester County District Attorney's Office, and using the street name of Frank Miranda, I was hired to drive a garbage truck by the widowed owner of a private carting company whose husband was shot to death, execution style. In an attempt to find her husband's killer, I chronicled an actual look into the private sanitation industry through the eyes of an undercover cop who lived it. It's also my emotional and psychological journey of the choices I had to make to do my job and at the same time maintain a relationship with the people I loved. Besides wanting to tell another police story that I've experienced, I want to tell people suffering from dyslexia, that with drive and determination, you can accomplish almost anything. I've struggled with dyslexia since I can remember. Meeting its challenges head on to write this book, and my first book, "Miranda Writes / Honor & Justice", has truly been one of the highlights of my life. To all the men and women in law enforcement, I say, "God bless you, and long live the police."

CHAPTER ONE

According to the Westchester County's Medical Examiner's Office, Leonard Capolla had been dead for several hours. Lividity had set in, or in laymen's terms, his blood had settled on the left side of his body where he landed when he fell. John Mercurio, who rented the apartment above Leonard's, stumbled upon his body in the early morning. It seemed that the killer or killers were pros. They'd unscrewed the overhead light bulb housed in a cheap circular fixture in the entry way, and laid in wait for him in the dark.

The police report indicated that Capolla had been shot twice in the back of the head with a small caliber pistol. His small-framed body was lying on its side in a fetal position. A pool of blood surrounded his body, oozing out of the jagged entry wound at the base of his skull. His eyes were open, staring into nothingness. The Medical Examiner concluded that he died instantly. Detectives working the case had to piece together his last hours, visiting the clubs he frequented, and the women he dated. His ex-wife was a person of interest, with money or revenge a possible motive.

As I read through the police reports, Capolla, age 46, had been divorced several years ago, had no children, and lived alone. Several of his girlfriends who were interviewed, said that he was a smooth talker, wore Gucci or Armani suits, carried a lot of cash, and was generous at spreading it around. Apparently robbery wasn't a motive. He had $1,500 in $100 bills, secured by a money clip, and stuffed in his pants pocket.

One of the girls said that he was self-conscious about his appearance, especially his thinning hair that he combed over the bald spot at the top of his head. Detectives found out that a girlfriend of his worked in a unisex beauty salon in Pelham, N.Y. She faithfully dyed his hair light brown, once a month, but it looked unnatural because there wasn't a strand of gray hair to equal his age. It didn't matter to Leonard whether a woman was single or married. If he liked her, he'd try to get her into the sack. Since Leonard was a womanizer, we had to consider jealousy as a possible motive for his murder.

Garbage Murders

Leonard Capolla was the co-owner of C & C Carting, a private sanitation company. The other owner was Gary Corso, son of Carmine Corso, who's also in the private carting business. It's well known that Carmine is a Capo in the Genovese Crime family. Carmine's so called 'legitimate' source of income comes from C & C Waste Management, but we in law enforcement know better. He's involved in drug trafficking, illegal gambling, and loansharking. It's a known fact that the private carting industry is controlled by organized crime. The respective crime families parcel off territories, and control pricing for commercial and residential pickups at will. In effect, they've established a monopoly in the industry. If a customer thinks that he's being charged too much for monthly pickups, and decides to solicit a price from another carting company, the other company will sucker the customer in, by bidding the job at a lower monthly price. After a time, the customer's rates are jacked up back to where they were or higher.

If you're thinking about going into the private sanitation business, think again. Once you open your doors for business, you're soon approached and told that if you want to continue to operate, a percentage of your business has to be kicked back to the crime family whose territory you're in. The percentage of tribute varies and is determined by the amount of business your company produces. If you refuse to get on board, your drivers are assaulted, your trucks are burned, and in some instances, they'll kill you.

The fact that Capolla was the business partner of Gary Corso could make his murder difficult to solve. If he wasn't killed because of a love affair, then perhaps his murder was mob related.

That afternoon, Westchester County Assistant District Attorney Zack Friedman and homicide detectives from the New Rochelle PD met with Gary Corso at his place of business on Gun Hill Road, in the Bronx. Friedman later told me that he and Detectives John Barry and Larry Straub arrived at C & C Carting around 4:00 P.M. Detective Straub pulled into the yard and parked his royal blue 2010 Crown Victoria in one of the spaces designated for personal vehicles. At the time, four or five garbage trucks were parked in the lot. Gary's office is a two story red brick building located at one end of the yard. A short distance away is another building that housed the trucks.

Friedman said that Gary peered from the window blinds while they made their way to his office on the second floor. Just so you know a little about Zack Friedman and our relationship, we go back a few years. In 2004, Zack was transferred from the DA's Narcotics Bureau to its Homicide Bureau. He's a play-by-the-rules guy, and is trusted by the law enforcement community at large. It's well known that he's a workaholic. Perhaps that's why he hasn't gotten married and raised a family. His father is a lawyer who practices in Manhattan, his mother is a physiotherapist who practices in Westchester. His parents met at Columbia University. After they married, they bought a home in Scarsdale, NY where Zack grew up and attended Scarsdale schools. Zack graduated with honors from Boston University. At 40, he's an intimidating figure. His rugged look gives him a leg up when he needs to play rough and tough with the knuckleheads he prosecutes.

I'm getting ahead of my story. My name is Detective Frank Santorsola. I work for the Westchester County District Attorney's Office, New York. Frank Miranda is my undercover street name. A few years ago, I was responsible for upsetting the political apple cart in the DA's office. Again, I'm getting ahead of my story.

Right after the attack on the World Trade Center in New York City, Zack and I worked together on a major heroin smuggling case involving a federal informant who, along with some other members of his family, were convicted of trafficking heroin into the New York metropolitan area for the Lucchese crime family. During our two years together, the informant maintained his innocence, and wanted me to help him prove it. Zack was one of the prosecutors cross-designated as an Assistant United States Attorney, prosecuting the case. I brought him irrefutable evidence that the United States government convicted an innocent man. Zack served at the pleasure of the District Attorney. To get involved meant putting his head on the chopping block. But get involved he did. Through insurmountable odds, we stood up against the establishment, and had the informant's federal conviction overturned. Only a negligible percent of convictions are reversed. During this investigation I uncovered corruption within the DEA, the US Attorney's Office, and in the very heart of the Westchester County District Attorney's Office. Fortunately for Zack and me, I beat the DA and her Chief of Detectives at their own game. But, I'll get into that later in the story. That investigation, literally led me into this story and on the ride of my life.

Zack said that he and the detectives entered the outer office. Gary's secretary was seated behind an olive colored metal desk. The office was paneled in cheap light brown faux wood from floor to ceiling. There was a window on each side of the front door, and an old air conditioner stuck in another window to the right of the secretary's desk overlooking Gun Hill Road. An old weathered oak arm-chair hugged the wall by the door. Gary's secretary, Christina, was tall, shapely, and in her early twenties. She had pierced eyebrows and a butterfly tattoo on her wrist. It made me wonder if she had a tramp stamp. Oh well, I'll never know.

Dressed casually in blue jeans and a grey cardigan sweater, she looked up from her computer to see who walked in. Gary slowly opened his door and walked out of his office, followed by Jimmy "Shorty" Newcomb, a very short white male who appeared to be in his early thirties. The detectives immediately identified themselves, as did ADA Friedman, showing their credentials. Zack told me later that Gary was agitated by their presence. The muscles in his face were drawn as he spat out, gritting his teeth, "I've been expecting you guys. Believe me; you're wasting your time. I had nothing to do with Lenny's murder."

Detective Barry snarled, "Of course not," glancing at Newcomb who was seething. Barry huffed, "Who's this guy?"

Newcomb looked unkempt. His long brown hair was dirty and he was in need of a bath. He couldn't have been any taller than 5 feet and weighed about 125 pounds. He was wearing five pounds of blue overalls and heavy work boots. Gary took a short breath, and then shouted loudly, "The guy is Jimmy Newcomb, my office manager!"

Newcomb was about to walk out of the office, but Detective Straub put his hand on Newcomb's chest, stopping him. With a sarcastic inflection he huffed, "Uh, where ya goin? Take a seat. We'll be talking to you in a minute."

Mind you, I got all this from Zack. They asked Gary to step back into his office, a mirror image of the outer office. Gary turned, and slowly walked back into his office, followed by Friedman and the detectives. Pointing to several chairs over by the far wall, Gary motioned for them to have a seat. Gary nervously sat down behind his desk, as he fidgeted with his hands he defiantly said, "I have nothing to say. I'm just as upset about Lenny's murder as anyone else. I have no idea who killed him or wanted him dead."

Gary, in his early thirties, didn't look Italian. He had a light complexion, light brown hair, hazel eyes, stood 5'11', and had a stocky build. It seemed that his lifestyle of indulging on fine food and wine had apparently caught up with him. Detective Straub, a hulk of a man, in his early 40's, stands five foot ten inches tall. His thinning brown hair is graying at the temples. Straub was wearing a cheap blue suit that needed a good tailoring and pressing. Straub looked down at Gary and asked him gruffly where he had been between midnight and four A.M. last night.

Gary grunted as he took a breath, and cried out, "Home in bed. C'mon, you can check with my wife! I had nothing to do with Lenny's death and have no reason to want him dead. We were making good money together!" Gary said they had an ironclad business contract that would not benefit him in any way in the event of Lenny's death.

Detective Barry, a slender, 34 year old Irishman, has sharp blues eyes and curly blond hair. He calmly asked "Well then, who did it, if you didn't?"

Gary sunk down and in a sullen tone said, "I said, I don't know!"

Friedman, listening intently as Detective Barry stood inches away from Gary's face, asked, "So who killed your partner, and why was he killed? Did his ex-wife have anything to do with his murder?"
Gary, his hands trembling, his face contorted, stood up. Annoyed by the inference that Lenny's ex-wife may have had something to do with his murder, screamed, "Uh, I don't fucking know! They parted ways amicably. He left her well-heeled and she's in a new relationship!"

Detective Barry continued to press Gary, jabbing his finger into Gary's chest, his Irish brogue booming, "Well if you didn't to it and you say that his wife didn't want him dead, then who the fuck killed him? We're gonna speak to his ex-wife, you can be assured of that!"

Gary knocked Barry's hand away. He slammed his fists on the top of the desk, knocking the reading lamp over. "I'm not saying another mother fucking word! I want to speak to my lawyer!"

Friedman, his voice resounding above the others commanded, "Stop the questioning!" At this point, everyone was standing. Friedman continued, "We are going to find out who killed Leonard Capolla and why. You can take that to the bank." Looking over at Straub and Barry, he motioned his head toward the door and said, "Let's get out of here." They then turned and walked out of Gary's office, as Gary slumped back down into his chair.

In the outer office, Jimmy Newcomb was on the phone. Detective Straub took the phone from his hand and place it back on the receiver. He then spun Newcomb around. "We got a few questions for you!"

Newcomb clenched his fists, and exploded, "That was my lawyer. You wanna talk to me, talk to my lawyer. You want to question me, fucking call my attorney!" Christina sat there frozen in silence. Detective Straub let Newcomb go, giving him a shove as they walked out of the office.

Zack knew that Capolla's murder was going to be difficult to solve. This was only the beginning, and we had a lot more work to do.

CHAPTER TWO

Denise MacKenzie and I had finally moved in together. We pooled our money and rented a one-bedroom walk up on the fifth floor on Sagamore Road in Bronxville, New York. I moved out of the shithole apartment I rented in the North Bronx, and was finally living like a human being. Bronxville is an upscale community in Southern Westchester, bordering the Bronx, just off the Bronx River Parkway. Denise was living in a rental apartment in Riverdale, an upper middle class section of the Bronx. Since I didn't own any furniture, she had her furniture moved into the apartment. She has great taste in decorating, and for the most part, the furniture is modern, in light tones.

From our living room windows, we can see the park below that butts up against the Bronx River, and the Parkway. The only downside is the constant hum of the traffic. In the spring and summer, people walk their dogs and picnic by the river that lazily flows through the Bronx into the East River in Manhattan. The location is great, and it's only twenty minutes by the Metro North train into Midtown Manhattan.

Denise's passion is geology. As you'll come to find out, she is a student of geophysics. On the walls in the hallway that lead to the bedroom, hang Denise's framed diploma from Columbia University, and a number of her framed photos of rock formations photographed on her many trips to the Southwest. She is a brilliant photographer.

As I said, the apartment is a far cry from the fleabag I lived in on Hughes Avenue in the Bronx. Since moving into this apartment, my mental attitude has changed for the better, especially knowing that Denise is here. We met a year or so ago at Jake's Bar & Grill in the Chester Heights section of New Rochelle. Jake's is a cop friendly bat and ball joint, owned by Jake McDonald. His son Sal is a NYPD cop who works in patrol out of the 46th precinct in the West Bronx. One of my partners, Detective Joe Nulligan, has been dating one of the barkeeps, Jessica Carbone, for some time. Joe and I have been friendly for years, and know we have each other's backs on the street. When he's not working, he's usually at Jake's having a few beers and keeping an eye on Jessica. Jake's is fashioned after an old Irish Pub. The bar has six beer taps. They pump so much beer that the kegs need replacing every few days. Behind the bar is a mirrored wall, lined with glass shelves, stocked with the finest Irish whiskey. Red Breast 21 is among my favorites.

One night about a year ago, I walked into Jakes. Denise was sitting at the bar. She happened to be drop dead gorgeous. I asked if I could buy her a drink. I was immediately captivated by her. I hadn't dated since my divorce, and frankly I was yearning for female companionship. A yearning this hot, beautiful woman satisfied. At five foot ten inches tall, with crystal green eyes, shoulder length wavy blond hair, she was stunning. I definitely wanted to get to know this woman better. I told her that I'd been divorced for almost two years and felt comfortable enough to tell her that my ex-wife has been giving me a hard time when it came to seeing my girls, Catie and Francesca. Denise seemed interested and asked their ages. I smiled, thinking how precious they are. "Catie is four and Francesca is seven."

As the weeks went by, I learned that she was a graduate student at Columbia University, and much to my trepidation, an exotic dancer at the Melody Club in South Yonkers. As soon as she graduated from high school, she came to New York City and got a job working at Starbucks. Minimum wage didn't cover her living expenses and tuition at Columbia. He small savings account ran dry. She faced the possibility of dropping out of school. A fellow student confided in Denise that she paid her way through Columbia by working at the Melody Club as an exotic dancer. After much consideration, and a few sleepless nights, Denise came head to head with her dilemma and auditioned for a job at the Melody Club. Her earnings from exotic dancing, a few student loans, and merit-based scholarships, enabled her to earn her way through Columbia, and receive her degree in geophysics.

Denise grew up in North Chicago. Her Aunt Margret raised her since Denise was abandoned by her mother at age 12. Denise's widowed mother couldn't handle the pressure of raising a child alone. She left Denise with her sister Margret. Denise doesn't really remember her father at all. Her aunt told her that he drank himself to death by the time she was three. To this day, Denise faithfully calls her aunt once a week and regularly sends her money to help her with living expenses. Now that she has received her degree, dancing at the Melody Club is a thing of the past. The only thing she enjoyed about it was the fabulous money she made.

She now works for the Shell Oil Company, Manhattan Division, in their oil Geosciences department. At twenty-five, she's presently the youngest executive trainee in her department. She's the most goal-oriented person I've ever met.

It wasn't long before Denise knew everything about my life. She knew it was eating away at me that Helen made it difficult for me to see my kids. Helen has taken me to Family Court many times trying to have the court lessen my visitation rights. In open court, Helen told the judge that I'm a bad influence on my girls because of the criminal element I investigate. I began to think that Helen was right and I stopped fighting to see them. It seemed that my two worlds were colliding.

Living the double life of an undercover cop, while trying to keep my head screwed on straight, seemed an impossible task. I'd been working in deep cover so long that I couldn't separate my danger zone from my comfort zone. I drank a lot to numb the confusion of both worlds. But in retrospect, how could I raise my daughters properly given the unpredictability of my job. Alcohol became my frequent companion. It seemed to relive the stress of leading a double life, dealing with wise guys, and hardcore drug dealers. After meeting Denise, I seemed to get it together. Now, I'm coping better with the separation from my girls. I can breathe a lot easier without constantly feeling the gnawing pain of not tucking my girls in at night. I guess my purpose in life was to become a cop and help make our society a better place.

Helen took me to Family Court so many times that she finally annoyed the judge. He saw that I was being unduly harassed by her. I was awarded more frequent visits with my girls.

The pressure brought to bear on me by the former D.A., to prevent me from investigating her corrupt political ally, had taken its toll. When summoned to her office for more badgering, I decided to secretly record her threats. I recorded her and her chief of detectives' conversation and turned the tape over to a reporter from the New York Times. Needless to say, the proverbial shit hit the fan and justice has prevailed. The D.A and her chief incriminated themselves and have been exposed for the corrupt people that they are. They are no longer privileged to work in the criminal justice system.

CHAPTER THREE

Denise must have heard the sound of the key turning in the lock. As soon as I opened the door, she came running over, throwing her arms around my neck and pressing herself tightly against me. "Frankie, it's all over the news! It's on the front page of the New York Post! District Attorney Annette Larson and Chief of Detectives Shawn Daniels resigned, criminal charges pending!"

"I know." My eyes locked directly with hers. "I've been dealing with the fallout all day."

Denise took hold of my hand and led me into the living room. She pulled me close, wanting to know every detail. "Uh, your name is plastered all over the news. Tell me about the recording. What's it all about?"

"I'll be right back."

I walked into the bedroom and placed my pistol on the nightstand, threw on sweats, and walked back into the living room. Denise had poured two glasses of wine and was sitting on the couch. I settled down next to her and grabbed a glass of Pinot Noir. "Um, well, you've heard me speak of Mike Baraka, the federal informant I was working with?"

Looking a bit puzzled, she replied, "Sure. Don't tell me that he's in the middle of all this?"

"He is," I continued. "After I helped him get his federal drug trafficking conviction overturned, some time had passed, and we hadn't spoken. One afternoon I was in the squad room, having a cup of coffee with Nulligan, when Mike called. I was just about to ask him how he was doing when he blurted out that he and Cindy were expecting a baby."

Denise leaned back, sinking into the couch, and replied, "The baby must be a year old by now?"

"Yeah."

"It's a boy, right?"

"Yes."

"Cindy seems to have no resentment toward you. It was you who put her father Nick Galgano in prison, wasn't it? With her father Nick in prison and no mother around, I'm sure it's hard."

"Well, she has Mike's mom for support. Afrah has accepted Cindy as a daughter –in-law, even though she's not Arabic."

Denise was drawn to my every word as she listened intently. "Mike loves you like a brother," she said with a slight smile.

I nodded yes, thinking that Nick was a Luchesse soldier, and how hard it was for me to infiltrate his crew. For a moment the thought of Nick and the double life I lived, tumbled through my mind. "Yeah, it's cool between us. Anyway, getting back to Mike's call, he told me that he has some information that I might be interested in. I was surprised to hear that. I told him I thought that he was all done with supplying information to law enforcement. He said he just thought that he could help."

Denise gently put her hand on my knee and asked, "What did you do?"

"I'll admit it, I was curious, so I asked him what he had. He tells me that a friend of his works as a DJ at Legs Up, a Manhattan night club run by a Bonanno solider, Johnny "Hoops" Castelluccio. Mike says that State Senator Williams and some of his cronies were sitting at a table the other night with Castelluccio eating and drinking."
Denise then put her hand up to her chin. "Senator Williams…..I think I've read about him."

"Well," I said, "Williams represents Southern Westchester and the North Bronx. Mike tells me that Castelluccio's been financing Williams's political campaigns from the beginning and now wants the senator to help him launder heroin trafficking money through Swiss bank accounts."

"What?" Denise's mouth hung open. She raised her voice and asked, "How does Mike's friend know this?"

Her eyes were centered on mine as I replied, "Williams is having an affair with one of the waitresses at the club and evidently she has loose lips. The best part is that Senator Williams was behind District Attorneys Larson's bid for New York City Mayor."

"So, what did you say?"

"I didn't say anything." I pulled the phone away from my ear and motioned for Nulligan to listen in. But all Joe heard was Mike asking if I was still on the line. In a hurried voice Mike asked, "Frank, are you interested in going after Williams?"

Denise's hand slid off me, she shook her head as if she understood what my answer would be. "Now it all fits. Of course, you were interested. So what did you do?"

"Honey, the only thing I could think of doing was to go after them. Besides you've read the newspaper." I reached for my glass of wine and took a sip.

She reached for her glass and asked, "So what did Nulligan say after you hung up?"

I chuckled. "Joe said that I must like sticking my face into a fucking buzz saw. He said that I was out of my mind for putting my career on the line."

Denise was sitting on the edge of the couch. Unable to contain her excitement she asked, "Then what?"

"I got up and gave Joe a faint nod as I walked into Captain Christopher's office. I told Christopher that I was going upstairs to see the chief and make his day."

The curiosity continued to build in Denise's face. "Um, so, did Christopher ask why you wanted to see Daniels?"

"No, he didn't. He didn't want to know."

"Daniels' secretary wasn't expecting me when I walked in. When she looked up and saw me, her demeanor changed from relaxed to uncomfortable. She knew that something was up and immediately buzzed Daniels, telling him that I was in his outer office. I didn't have to wait long. The intercom buzzed and I heard him tell Jennifer, in his irritable gruff voice, to send me in. When I walked in, he glared at me with distain, but held his temper. I took the liberty and sat down. There was no hello. There was no, *What can I do for you Frank?* Without warning, he said harshly, *What do you want, Santorsola?* When I told him that I'd just gotten off the phone with Mike Baraka, you should have seen the expression on his face. The tight ass looked like he was going to pass out."

Denise chuckled. "Sorry Frankie, I don't mean to laugh, but you called him tight ass. I've never heard a person described that way before."

I started to laugh, too, and took another sip of wine. I took her hand and said, "I guess it's funny now, but it wasn't then. Hey, you wanna hear more bull shit?" Still giggling, she shook her head yes.

I took a short breath. "So then numb nuts grabbed the bottle of Pepto Bismol sitting on his desk and started slugging it down his throat."

"Oh my God."

"So what happened next?"

"The overbearing prick was speechless. He doesn't let anyone talk for long, but I guess he didn't know what to say. I caught him off guard, taking the offensive, and telling him that Senator Williams is in bed with Johnny Castelluccio. I said that Castelluccio wants Williams to launder heroin money through a Swiss bank account. I ranted on and said, "Chief, I'd like to open a case to investigate the allegations.""

"What did he say?"

"By now he was a livid. He leaned over his desk, squinting through his glasses, and told me not to do a fucking thing. I couldn't believe it. He jumped up and stormed out of the office, leaving me sitting there. I sat thinking that I hoped he'd have a heart attack in the hallway and croak. After a few seconds, I got up, closed the door behind me, and winked at Jennifer as I left."

Denise hung on my every word. "Wow! What were you thinking? Were you scared? "

"Yeah, I was scared. I threw a lot of shit in the game. Daniels and DA Larson had wanted to get rid of me ever since they ordered me to sever ties with Mike Baraka, and I didn't. Mike was right all along about a DEA agent running an international heroin trafficking ring. That information led me to proving his innocence of heroin trafficking, and ultimately having his federal conviction overturned."

Denise looked shocked and said, "Oh my."

"Yeah, oh my. My investigation of Williams would throw a monkey wrench into Larson's political aspirations of becoming the next Mayor of New York City. Its common knowledge that Senator Williams is championing Larson's run for mayor and lobbying for money to finance her war chest. So, without a doubt, Larson had to find a way to muzzle me."

"Where did Daniels go? What did he do?" she asked as she offered her hand.

"He went straight to the District Attorney."

"What happened then?"

"When I walked back into the squad room, Nulligan walked over to me, wondering how it went with the chief. I gave him a look as if to say, you gotta be kidding me. I told Joe that the chief told me not to do a fucking thing, and then ran out of his office. The next thing I know my phone rings, and it's Daniels. He said that he and Larson wanted me in her office immediately, and slammed down the phone. Joe knew that the call was from Daniels, and asked what I was going to do. I didn't say anything. I took a small digital audio recorder from my desk drawer, and stuck it in the inside pocket of my sport jacket. I winked at Joe, and as I walked out, I heard Joe say, "Fuck em!"

Denise was now animated, talking with her hands. "Gees Frankie, how can you cope with people like Larson and Shawn Daniels? Isn't it enough that your undercover work takes you into a world where you have to deal with all sorts of criminals? It's really sad to find out that the people, sworn to protect us, are no better than the people you've put away."

I nodded sadly. "Yeah, it's fucked up. Anyway, before I walked into Larson's office I made sure that the recorder was turned on. Larson's secretary, Gloria, immediately buzzed me in. You know, Larson's only in her mid forties and in her second term of office. She thinks she's got everybody fooled, but she never fooled me. When you hear those high heels clicking down the hallway, you had better run for cover. Don't let her petite stature, glasses, and youthful complexion fool you. She has a manipulative edge and is vicious. Larson can spew the most poisonous venom at anyone who gets in her way."

Denise was nervously biting her lip as she sat there. "Um, well, what did they say when you walked in?"

"Well, the chief was standing next to Larson. He was pacing back and forth, and charged me to sit down. His tone was abrupt, his contempt for me written all over his face. I guess they thought that I was the proverbial lamb being lead to slaughter. But they were wrong. They underestimated me. They didn't think I'd be recording them."

Denise pointed to a photograph on the table in the entry way. "Is that Daniels?"

"Yes." I replied. "The photo was taken after a golf outing at Winged Foot Golf Club in Larchmont, New York. It's Daniels, me, and a few of the guys."

"Frankie, is that what he really looks like?"

I thought for a moment and laughed, "Yeah, that's him with the sagging mound of skin under his neck."

"So, what was said next?"

"Then the verbal double teaming began. Larson started first. She said that Senator Williams was a good friend, and that she didn't care who he decided to have dinner with, or what he's alleged to be involved in. Her lambasting seemed to be endless. She raised her voice saying that her office would never investigate him regardless of what a low-life informant alleged. Chief Daniels jumped in, raising his voice and said that he ordered me to sever ties with Baraka, months ago, and that I can't get it through my Guinea head to stay away from him. He roared on that I've been a thorn in his side since I was assigned to the squad. The tape recording rolled on as he threatened me. He said that if I didn't resign, he would see to it that I'd be shot in the line of duty by friendly fire."

In sync with Daniels tirade, Larson raged on, "Frank, I don't have to go through a litany of the power brokers I know. Do I? If you don't resign, I'll destroy you. You won't know what hit you. I'm on my way to becoming Mayor of New York City, and nothing or nobody, especially a burnt out cop is going to get in my way!"

Denise jumped up from the couch, emotionally charged, shouting, "Frankie, you got them! You got them! The newspaper said that the Governor is appointing a new DA until a special election can be held, and he's appointing a special prosecutor to handle the criminal charges!" Denise plopped back down on the couch, pressing her face against mine. She whispered, "Frankie, I love you. Please don't let anything happen to you."

I stroked her hair and looked into her eyes, and told her that I that I wasn't going to let anything happen to me. We held the embrace for a moment and kissed passionately. We were both sexually on fire and about to go into the bedroom when Joe called.

"Frankie, its Joe. I got some bad news. You better sit down."

"What is it Joe?"

"Are you sure you're sitting down?"

"C'mon Joe. I got things to do. Don't fuck around."

"Okay, Okay. I just heard from Sergeant Steve Skowronski that Deputy Chief Howell has just been appointed acting chief until a new chief is named."

I walked in circles as I listened. "Joe, you mean we gotta deal with Shake-N- Bake?"

"Yeah, we gotta deal with him."

Joe was eager to tell me more, but I was tired and wanted to go to bed. I tried to hurry him off the phone, but he wouldn't take a hint. "Frankie, there's more. The skinny is that the Governor has appointed a new DA. The rumor is that the new guy has already lined you up with a case."

That got my attention.

"Joe, who did the Governor appoint, and what's the case?"

"The guys name is John Xavier Hogan. He comes out of the Security Exchange Commission, and from what I hear, he's a fair guy."

"Joey, what's the investigation?"

 "I don't know, but I guess that you'll find out tomorrow."

I paused for a split second, thinking about what he just said. "Okay, Joey. Thanks for the heads up. See ya tomorrow."

As soon as I hung up, Denise wanted to know what the call was about.

"Nulligan heard that the Governor has just appointed a new district attorney, and that the new DA was assigning me to an investigation." She had a worried look on her face, but didn't say anything. I took her hand and said with a slight smile, "It will all work out. It's late. Let's go to bed."

CHAPTER FOUR

The office had recently issued me another confiscated car, seized from a drug dealer. It replaced the old Pontiac Firebird that I'd been driving. I'd been assigned a 2002 candy apple red Chevy Corvette hard top, with a black leather interior. Captain Larry Christopher, my squad commander made sure I got the car. It's got all the bells and whistles and doesn't have cop written all over it. It's registered under my fictitious name, Frank Miranda, 1425 Hughes Avenue Bronx, New York. I guess it's one of the perks for risking your life.

Acting Chief Howell called me earlier in the morning. He told me to be in the office at 10:30 A.M. to meet the new DA. It's the DA's first day in the office and I couldn't imagine why he wanted to see me before introducing himself to the entire staff. I decided to get into the office early and try to find out about my new assignment. I arrived in White Plains about 8:00 A.M. and parked in underground garage of the Westchester County Court House. I'm cleared to park in a restricted area, reserved for squad detectives and the District Attorney. I walked off the elevator and headed for the squad room, saying hello and talking with a few of the assistant district attorneys who were on their way to court. I had a feeling that they wanted to talk about Annette Larson's resignation, but they didn't go there.

After several minutes of polite conversation, I continued down the corridor to the squad room where forty or so detectives make up the DA's police force. They are assigned to the various investigative bureaus headed by an assistant district attorney who reports directly to the 2nd Deputy District Attorney.

The squad room holds forty plus battleship gray desks, separated by a center isle. Half the desks are positioned on one side of the isle and half on the other side. It's illuminated by recessed lighting that gives the room a sterile look. At the far end of the room is Captain Larry Christopher's office. He's recently been assigned to run the narcotics squad. Larry just turned forty-six. He's tall and solidly built, with fair skin, blue eyes and light blond hair. It's a product of his Irish DNA. Larry usually dresses casually in blue jeans, a polo shirt, and he carries his sidearm in a shoulder holster. The detectives in the unit respect him. It's safety first, and the investigation second. His desire is that his detectives go home to their families at the end of the day. Larry's demeanor is calm and he talks to his subordinates with respect. However, when push comes to shove, he can make his point.

When I walked in, Joe Nulligan was sitting at his desk reading the newspaper and drinking a cup of coffee. I tapped him on the shoulder as I slid behind him to get to my desk. He looked up at me, cocked his head and said. "I didn't expect you in so soon."

A few detectives were milling around bullshitting, while others were banging out police reports on their computers. Angel Serrano was on his cell phone, over by the paper shredder scolding his divorce lawyer. Serrano, who is animated anyway, was waving his arms wildly and talking so loudly that he could be heard in the hallway. A few of the guys asked him to keep a lid on it. Angel is no one to fool with. He'd be the first one to get up into your face if he didn't like what you said. He grunted, raised his free hand, leveled his middle finger at ninety degrees, and shot everyone the bird as he continued his call. You've gotta laugh, these guys are real, there's no pretense, and they tell it like it is.

I looked at a few personal messages that were scattered on my desk. Joe and I discussed the new DA and all the shit in the paper about Larson and Daniels resigning. Nulligan and I met as cadets in the police academy. We hit it off from the very beginning. We also laugh at the same things. I hate to admit it, but we usually laugh at other people's expense, most of the time. In his late thirties, he stands out in a crowd. He's five feet ten inches and 215 pounds. Joe's hair is reddish blonde. His deep-set blue eyes can put the fear of God in anyone who pisses him off. He's a guy who'd rather run head on through his difficulties than calmly think through them. We got together socially when we were both married men, but since our divorces, we haven't double dated. Its funny, but most cops feel comfortable socializing with other cops. I guess it's easier. We can be ourselves, and talk and laugh about the job. On the other hand, I can't tell you how many times I've been approached at a party by someone who found out that I was a cop, and asked if I could fix a parking ticket. I'd be polite and say that the tickets are routinely scrutinized by my sergeant, so unfortunately, I can't help them.

Over the years, I've been assigned to work deep undercover cases for long periods of time, meeting sporadically with a squad detective on the street to hand over reports and covert recordings. I'd infiltrated an organized crime crew running numbers and a sports betting business. At the same time, Joe was doing his own thing in the narcotics squad. He was partnered up with Angel Serrano. I trusted Angel with my life and felt good about them working together.

Angel is a street-wise detective who grew up in the South Bronx. His parents had moved to the states from Mayaguez, a small town in Puerto Rico, when he was ten. Reminiscing over the years, Angel fondly recalls community pig roasts on an open pit where everyone in the town celebrated. He shared that one of his best childhood memories was Christmas Eve with his family at Nuestra Senora de la Candelaria Cathedral in Mayaguez. His strict upbringing kept him on the straight and narrow. Angel is bi-lingual. It gives him an edge up on developing informants. He's credited with making solid narcotic cases that hold up in court. Angel looks more like a school teacher than a cop. He's forty, short, round, and baby faced. His olive complexion is silky-smooth and belies his age.

After Angel had enough of his attorney's bullshit, he clicked off his phone. After forcefully shoving his phone in his pocket, he muttered a few inaudible curses and walked over. "You guys know what it's like. The ex-wife never leaves you alone. They're like a case of herpes. It never goes away."

Joe looked at Angel as if sharing the same feelings. "You got that right, Angel. They won't leave you alone until they throw dirt in your face."

I glanced at Joe and then back at Angel, and said, as I thought about my marriage to Helen, "It's funny Angel, in the beginning you can't live without each other. Then things change."

"Yeah, Frankie it's too bad, but life goes on. I finally met a nice girl at the Puerto Rican Day Parade in Manhattan. As it turned out, we went to the same grammar school in Mayaguez. Marla cooks all of the Puerto Rican dishes better than my mother. I love the way she makes fried plantains and tarts filled with shrimp and rice. Her chicken and rice, and chorizo sausage with garbanzo beans are the best. What I love most of all, is the way she roasts pork. She lets the pig skin get crispy brown just the way I like it. And besides being a great cook, the girl's hot and I don't mean only in the kitchen. By the way guys, I heard that the new DA is upstairs. The skinny is that he's got Frank lined up for something. Do you know what it is, Frankie?"

I shrugged my shoulders and shook my head and said, "No, I haven't a clue. I can't believe he wants to see me before introducing himself to the entire office."

Angel sighed. "No doubt he's going to talk to you about the Larson and Daniels thing."

Joe put his coffee down, rubbed his chin, probably thinking about what Angel just said. "Whatever it is, pal, know that you'll be up to your eyeballs in alligators."

I shook my head, nodding in agreement and said, "I guess it's time for me to head upstairs." I was nervous about meeting the new DA and anxious about not knowing what I was walking into. I've heard about him over the years. He prosecuted some high profile insider trading cases for the Security Exchange Commission. His family is politically connected. He married into a wealthy family. His wife, C.J. Rollins, is the daughter of John Rollins, the former Governor of Ohio. The story goes that he's using the DA's office as a stepping stone for higher office.

I gave Angel and Joe a wink as I walked out of the squad room. The uniformed police officer seated outside Hogan's office recognized me as I approached. He glanced up from his newspaper. "They're expecting you detective. Go right in."

The duty officer was big and burly. I'm sure he could take care of any problem that might come his way. I opened the large mahogany door, and walked into Hogan's outer office. His secretary, Corrine, looked up from her computer, shyly smiling, and in a soft voice said, "Oh, hi Detective Santorsola, DA Hogan is expecting you, go right in."

Corrine buzzed the door open. My eyes were immediately drawn to the new District Attorney, who was standing behind his desk; the desk that Annette Larson, recently occupied. A handsome man, in his late thirties, he stood six feet tall with blonde hair neatly combed back. His dark blue eyes were intimidating. He dressed in a blue Brooks Brothers suit, a red and blue striped tie, and Dubarry shoes. His initials, JXH, were monogrammed on his shirt cuffs. He looked like he could be on the cover of GQ. I noticed his Georgetown Law diploma on the walnut podium that his predecessor used many times during her flamboyant press conferences.

I had a suspicion that the acting chief would attend the meeting, but I was surprised to see Zack Friedman, and a man and woman in their early thirties that I didn't know. They were all seated in front of Hogan. I walked up to Hogan and he extended his hand, as did I. "Frank, it's nice to finally meet you. Please sit. Sorry for the impromptu meeting." I sat in an empty chair between Friedman and Howell. The couple sat to Howell's right.

Hogan was charismatic and had a take-charge attitude. By his tone, he seemed excited to meet me. "Frank, it's nice to finally meet you. I've heard a lot about your escapades."

"Um well, it's nice to meet you as well, Mr. Hogan."

I immediately glanced over at the two people sitting to my far right. They looked over and nodded. The guy's head was bandaged. He was casually dressed in blue jeans, brown loafers, and a cream colored Polo sports shirt, with an expensive gold Rolex hanging off his wrist. The woman was a slim, dark haired beauty. She was smartly dressed in a light blue blouse, blue jeans, a diamond encrusted Rolex, and black stilettos with red soles. I couldn't help but notice the red soles because of the way she sat, crossing her ankles. From the corner of my eye, I saw her head turn to get a look at me. Hogan looked over at the Corso's and then turned to me and said, "Frank, everyone met the Corso's earlier. I'd like you to meet Gary and his wife, Dana."

I smiled. "Nice to meet you."

The DA focused his attention directly on me. He said that the Corso's had come to this office for help. In a pressing voice he remarked, "Detective Santorsola, I'm sure you couldn't help but notice that Mr. Corso has been injured. He was shot a few weeks ago. Have you heard anything about the shooting?"

"No sir. I haven't."

"Frank, Mr. Corso owns a private sanitation company in the Bronx. He has moved his company to a facility in West New Rochelle after the shooting. He was shot while speaking to one the drivers in the maintenance garage. Two men wearing ski masks walked in brandishing handguns and began firing. It happened so quickly, he barely got a look at the shooters. Fortunately for Mr. Corso, he was able to dive under one of the trucks, which saved his life. The gunmen continued to fire. The bullets ricocheted off the floor, grazing his head. As you can see, he escaped serious injury. Detectives from the 47th precinct in the Bronx are working the case."

I glanced over at Gary, his facial expression was painful. He grimaced as Hogan spoke. I sat up, looking directly at Gary. "Mr. Corso, I'm sorry for your trouble. You're lucky that you survived."

Hogan cleared his throat to get everyone's attention, "Zack, will you go on and brief Detective Santorsola as to why he's here."

"Yes sir. Last month, Mr. Corso's partner, Leonard Capolla, was murdered in his home in New Rochelle. New Rochelle detectives are investigating his homicide and so far they have no leads."

Chief Howell, who had to justify his importance, interrupted clamoring, "Uh, whoever killed Gary's partner knew what they were doing. They left no forensic evidence at the scene."

I looked over at Howell thinking that he's the only one left standing after the untimely departure of DA Larson and her chief. Thinking, how ridiculous he is. He's fifty years old and couldn't make a decision to throw water on his balls if they were on fire. He's jokingly referred to in the squad as Shake-N-Bake. He perspires and sometimes needs a change of clothes when things get rough. Howell spends a lot of his time studying for the next promotional exam to advance his career. Everyone knows that he's only in job for the money and benefits and not to serve and protect our community to make it a better place to live.

Friedman continued and said, "Since the Capolla murder, the drivers of Mr. Corso's company have been threatened and assaulted on their routes. They've been told to stay off the trucks, or else."

Hogan's posture stiffened. His voice was assertive, "Frank, that's where you come in."

I leaned forward, not really understanding what he meant. I was wide-eyed and surprised. "I don't understand? How do I fit in with all this? I'm assigned to narcotics, not homicide."

Hogan pointed his index finger at me and said, "Frank, you've worked closely with Zack in the past and I think that you're the right fit for this assignment. I've taken a hard look at your record and I like what I see. We want you to start driving a garbage truck for the Corso's. With any luck, you might find out who's behind the assaults, the attempt on Gary's life, and maybe who killed Leonard Capolla."

I thought, me drive a garbage truck? That's ridiculous, what are they thinking? It will take me months to learn how to operate a garbage truck.

Friedman noticed the expression on my face. He saw that I was uncomfortable with the assignment. He delicately interrupted, "Frank, I know that you're concerned about driving the truck, but you'll learn as you go. We know that it will take time, but you'll have a helper riding along."

Howell had to stick his two cents in. His eyeglasses sat on the edge of his nose, as he said, "Frank, we know you can pull this off."

I rolled my eyes with a distrustful smirk, but didn't say anything.

The Corso's sat there quietly, with an expression of abject hopelessness etched on their faces. I could almost hear their hearts pounding. They were looking for a way out of the dangerous mess they were in. In desperation, Gary sat upright in the chair, and pleaded, "Detective Santorsola, we don't know who else to turn to. You know who my father is, but I don't want his kind of help. It will only get me in more trouble than it's worth. You gotta know that I built the business up from nothing. I bought the route from my father three years ago and it was barely making a profit. Now that it's making money, somebody out there wants to take it away from me."

Dana Corso, sitting on the edge of her chair, looked as if she was about to cry. She said, "Please detective, we came to the DA's office for help. I knew that this office was the one to come to."

Looking directly at the Corso's, I was about to say something when Howell interrupted me. I held my hand up abruptly. "Hold it." Turning back to the Corso's, I wanted to make sure they knew where I was coming from and that there wasn't any misunderstanding between us. "Huh, it looks like I'll be driving for you, but you gotta know that my butt is on the line here. Gary's father is a Capo in the Genovese family. He's got a reputation for hurting people. If the wrong people find out that I'm on the truck, my life is in jeopardy. You get my drift? "

"Yes detective. I know. I know all about him, his life, and how he makes a living. Like Dana said, I didn't go to my father for help. I came to Mr. Hogan. As a matter of fact, I told my father that I didn't want his help. So, you don't have to worry about Dana and me. No one will know that you're a cop but us. Dana's eyes were burning into me. She hung on every word her husband said. Then with an inflection in her voice she said, "The best thing my father-in-law can do is to stay out of it."

Chief Howell sounded off, trying his hardest to be authoritative. "Okay, it's settled then. Frank you'll start in a few days. The only people that'll know that you'll be driving for the Corso's are in this room. Even Gary's attorney won't know. And by the way, you're being assigned another car, a 1998 Cadillac Eldorado. After all, driving a Corvette won't fit your new image."

I sat there thinking that Howell can't help himself. He's such a jerk. What a miserable excuse for a human being. I knew he was looking for a reaction, but I didn't give him the satisfaction.

Hogan looked totally satisfied with the way the meeting went and reiterated his sentiments. "Gentlemen, it's settled then. Frank, for now you'll report directly to Chief Howell and Friedman will monitor the investigation from my end. The only people in the squad that will know of your assignment are on a need to know basis. Now, if there are no other questions, we can conclude the meeting."

As everyone stood to leave, Hogan buzzed his secretary, asking her to come in and escort the Corso's to the elevator. I had a few questions for Gary before he left. I walked up to him. "Hey Gary, I need to know a few things before you leave."

"Sure detective."

"Call me Frank."

"Okay, Frank."

"What time in the morning do I start?"

With a good natured smile he replied, "We roll out at 3:00 A.M."

I thought to myself, holy shit, now I have to get up at 1:00 in the morning?

Gary must have noticed the expression on my face and his grin grew wider. In a business like voice, he said, "The yard's on Fourth Street between Sickles Avenue, and Union Avenue. You'll be picking up commercial stops emptying containers from ten to a hundred and fifty yards. It varies. You'll have a guy to operate the hopper. His name is Louis Fuganza. We call him Nutsey."

"Nutsey?"

"Yeah, he'll show you how to hook up the winch to the containers. Don't worry Frank, you'll be okay." I stood there shaking my head, not really knowing what to say. "By the way, when can you start?"

I paused for a second and said, "I'll need a day to take care of some personal things. So let's start Monday. And, from now on my name is Frank Miranda. I'll fax over my phony identification for your payroll records."

"That will work." He said with a sigh of relief. "Okay Frank, I'll see you on Monday."

I was thinking that the yard is only a couple of miles from Jake's Bar & Grill, so I'll have to make sure that I'm not followed there after work.

Corrine stood by the door, motioning for the Corso's to follow her out to the public elevator. It was then that Hogan asked that the rest of us stay for a minute. His eyes seemed to brighten as he sat back down. I guess partly from the success of the meeting and partly because it was his first day as the new district attorney. He said enthusiastically, "People, thanks for your time. I want you to know that I plan to introduce myself to the entire staff later this afternoon. We'll meet in the large Grand Jury room down on the third floor. I plan to speak about my philosophy in running this office and what's expected of each and every one of you. I expect one hundred and ten percent from my staff. As we all know there's a dark cloud that hangs over the office due to the alleged criminal conduct of my predecessor and her chief of detectives. This morning the Governor called informing me that former DA Larson and Shawn Daniels have been indicted by a State Grand Jury. They've been charged with obstruction of justice, official misconduct, coercion, and extortion. We all know that these charges stem from the recorded conversation Frank made and his testimony. They're out on bail awaiting trial."

I thought, wow! I did all that. It's really hard to wrap my head around it all. What if it had gone the other way? What if Larson hadn't summoned me to her office and instead decided to set me up with contraband, or worse, go through a door with shooters on the other side? A la Frank Serpico. There'd be no recording. No threats. No criminal conduct. I'd be fucked right now, maybe even dead. The thought of it made my insides crawl. Zack noticed that I was out of sorts. "Frankie, are you alright?" Of course Howell could give a shit less about how I looked or felt. He sat there not saying a word. His only interest is in how far he can get his nose up Hogan's ass. We all know that his goal is to be appointed the next permanent chief, at any expense.

I took a deep breath, replying to Zack's concern, "I'm okay."

As Howell stood to leave, his eyes were riveted on me. Taking his best shot, at being a leader, he muttered, "Well Frank, take a few days off before you start your assignment. So, if Mr. Hogan is finished, let's go."

Hogan extended his hand, first to me, then to Zack and then to Howell. "Gentlemen, thank you. And, Frank, good luck. It's important for this office to begin a new chapter in law enforcement." Slightly nodding his head and smiling, he winked at me as we walked out of his office.

No sooner than we walked out into the hallway, Howell told me that he wants to see me in his office. He told Friedman that it won't be necessary for me to attend the staff meeting. Howell said that my reports will go directly to him. Friedman raised his eyebrows looking surprised, but nodded in agreement. He didn't want to be on Howell's bad side now that he was acting chief. Before walking away, Zack patted me on the shoulder and said, "Frank, we'll talk soon. And please call me if you need anything."

I shot Howell *a what's this all about* look and replied, "I will Zack. You can count on it." Howell noticed my gesture, giving me a dirty look as we walked down the hall and into his office. It's the same office that Shawn Daniels occupied.

His secretary, Jennifer Williams, was pounding away on her computer as we walked in. Jennifer once worked for Shawn Daniels. Now that Howell is the acting chief, her loyalties lie with him. This chick knows how to play the political ball game. She's tall, shapely, single, and at thirty-five, I'd love to know who's bedding her. Her soft white skin tones and shoulder length black hair give her a sultry look. She was dressed smartly, wearing a dark blue skirt, a sweater, with a monogrammed necklace. It was rumored that Shawn Daniels was probably banging her, but that has never been confirmed. Now that he's out of the picture, I'm sure she has a new squeeze tucked away somewhere. Jennifer looked up as we walked in and asked politely, "Chief is there anything you need?"

Howell walked in with his head pointed down towards the floor, and replied, "No Jennifer. I have to speak with Frank. Please see to it that we're not disturbed." The jackass didn't even have the courtesy to look at her when he spoke. He rushed into his office, with me following behind. "Frank, sit down."

I slid the chair in front of his desk. He paused a moment while rummaging through his desk, apparently looking for something. It was like *dejavu*. I've been in the hot seat before. Only this time, it's in front of Howell instead of Shawn Daniels. The only addition to the office was the books shelves that lined the back wall. They were filled with his personal collection of books, General Schwarzkopf's, *It Doesn't Take a Hero*, among his favorites.

He pulled out a legal size folder from one of the desk drawers, and threw it down in front of him. As I sat there waiting to be filleted, I noticed a picture of his wife, who looked like she's been down a long hard road. I guess there is someone for everyone. He fumbled through the folder for a moment, and then he finally looked at me. I had a feeling he wanted to set me straight about something. One thing was for sure, I wasn't sitting here because he was lonely. Pointing to the file, he said, "Frank, all your police reports will be kept in this folder and the file will be locked in my safe. The investigation number I'm assigning is 2004-150."

I asked, "What about Friedman's reports?"

The nasty son of a bitch snapped at me. "That's not your concern! I'll take care of Friedman. Just know that what happened to Shawn Daniels isn't going to happen to me. Whenever we talk, I'm going to make sure you're not wearing a wire. Got that! And remember, Frank, you work for me now! Oh, and like I said, don't forget to leave the Corvette down stairs. We wouldn't want anyone to see a garbage man driving a Corvette, now would we?"

I sat up. I wanted to strangle the cocksucker, but I knew better. Using every bit of self control I had, I sat there with the biggest burn and answered calmly, "No John, we wouldn't want to see a garbage man driving a Corvette, now would we. You just make sure I get the support I need and we won't have a problem. You got it?"

He lost it, shouting, "Remember what I said. I run the show now, Santorsola, and you had better tow the line or I'll have you walking a foot post in the projects. Now get out of my office!"

I stood, staring at him for a second, and then said, "With pleasure chief."

As I started for the door, I looked back. The old wind bag stood there grimacing, and huffing and puffing. When I got to the fourth floor, Joe and Angel were in the squad room. I'm sure that they were waiting for me to fill them in on my meeting with Hogan.

Joe asked curiously, "Frankie, so what's up with Hogan, and how did it go?"

Angel, working at his desk across the isle from Joe looked over. "C'mon Frankie, what's going on?"

Captain Christopher, also curious, walked out of his office and tossed me the keys to the Cadillac. "It's parked downstairs."

I reluctantly reached into my pants pocket for the keys to the Corvette, tossing them back to him as I huffed, muttering a few inaudible curses. "Huh, some things never change around here." Looking over at Captain Christopher, then glancing back at Angel and Joe, I said, "Guys, all I can say is that I'm out of narcotics for a while. I've been assigned to the homicide bureau."

Captain Christopher understood that Shake-N-Bake didn't want him in the loop, and I guess he didn't care. He had enough going on.

Joe was offended. "C'mon Frankie what's the big fucking deal."

Angel looked over at me, as if I'd slapped him in the face. "Yeah, what's the big fucking secret? The new DA doesn't trust us?"

It was difficult for me to listen to them. "Ah, come on guys. I was told it's on a need to know basis."

I stood in the center isle not knowing what else to say. Joe and Angel just sat there with a look of betrayal. I turned to Joe, and said, "I'll be taking some days off before I start my new assignment. Guys, I won't be coming into the office until this thing is over." Joe and Angel sensed not to ask me any more questions. I spent a few more minutes in the squad room and then headed for the side exit.

Nulligan shouted, "Frankie, be safe. If you need anything call me."

I yelled back, "I will Joey. Thanks."

I took the stairwell to the basement. In the garage I looked around and finally spotted an old beat up yellow Cadillac sitting over in the corner. I'm thinking to myself, here we go again. I just got fucked and Howell didn't use Vaseline. I walked to the car and got in. The car smelled musty, and I'm thinking, if this car could talk, it could tell some fantastic stories of the roads it's travelled and the people who've owned it. I turned the key. The car sputtered and started. I drove out of the parking structure onto Martin Luther King Boulevard, headed for the Bronx River Parkway, driving south, to Bronxville. I asked myself, *who's behind the attempt on Gary's life. Can I pull off driving a garbage truck?* One thing is for sure, Hogan struck me as a man who will bring positive changes to the office. I am the first experiment in his vision for Hogan's *Camelot.*

CHAPTER FIVE

I called Helen and asked about taking the girls for a few days. They haven't met Denise yet, and I knew that once I started the undercover assignment, I wouldn't be seeing my girls much.

Denise walked into the apartment at 7:30 P.M. after arriving by cab from the Bronxville train station. She noticed that I was upset and asked, "Ah, Frankie, what's wrong? Is everything alright?"

"I just off got the phone with Helen; I asked to pick up the kids for a few days, but she said no. She said that I didn't give her enough notice. I tried to explain that I have a few days off and wanted to see them. She said that I only fit them into my life when it's convenient for me, and that my job has always comes first. I begged her and told her that my mom was missing the kids. Besides, I said, if it weren't for my job, she wouldn't be getting child support and alimony payments. Did I tell you that last year she called my office to say that I'd threatened her and the kids with my gun? The woman tried to get me fired."

Denise walked over, gently wrapped her arms around my neck, and pulled me close. We were eye to eye, our lips nearly touching. "Frankie I'm so sorry."

"Me too, it hurts." My eyes welled up with tears.

Denise gently pushed herself away and said, "I really wish I could help. I wish that there was something I could do."

I pulled her close to me, whispering gently, "I wish there was something you could do too, but there isn't. I'll just have to live with it."

She softly stroked my face, and kissed me. I held her tightly, kissing her tenderly. She slowly pulled me towards the sofa. While removing her suit jacket, she unbuttoned her blouse, letting them fall to the floor. Seductively she unhooked her bra, exposing her breasts. She began to breathe hard as I gently kissed her lips. Suddenly the thought of Catie and Francesca flashed through my mind, and I stopped. I just couldn't make love to her now. I slowly pushed her away as our eyes were locked on each others and said, "I'm sorry, I can't." She was still breathing heavily. She pressed her body against mine and kissed my lips. "I understand darling." As she walked away the house phone rang. "It's your mother, Frankie, and by the way, since you have a few days off, I know of a nice hotel in Providence that we can escape to."

"Tell her I'll be right there." I picked up the phone in the hallway. I knew that my mother was about to hit me with her usual guilt trip. "Hi Ma, how are you?"

She spoke in broken English, speaking to me as if she had been wounded. "I no hear from you in a couple-a days-a. Quando lo io incontrare lei?"

"Ma, you'll meet her soon."

"Why you no call? Coma esti Franco?"

She's knows how to push the right buttons to make me and my brother feel guilty. The best thing I could do was not to feed into the trap and agree with everything she has to say. So I replied, "I'm fine ma. Sorry, I've been busy."

Then, laying the ultimate guilt trip on me, and sounding like a wounded bird, she said, "Uh, how's-a Catie and Francesca? When I see dem?"

Trying to lighten the mood I said, "Soon Ma. You'll see them soon. I asked Helen for the kids. I had a few days off, but she said no. My days off don't fit in with my scheduled visitation."

My mom mumbled something in Italian, then with a tone of condemnation she sighed, "It's –a- no right. You da father. Helen should- a let you see dem. She knows-a what you job is."

"Ma, I've been all through it. I know."

"Good- a thing you father is gone."

"Yeah Ma. Good thing. "

Then she trailed off, probably thinking about my marriage to Helen. "How's- a- you girl friend? She a treats you nice?"

I was intent not to discuss my relationship with Denise. She would meet her soon enough. Besides, we just moved in together and I wanted to make sure that we were really going to be a couple, especially before she met my mother. "Yeah, Ma. She's terrific. She wants us to get away for a few days. I think it's a good idea."

"It's you birthday, where you go?"

"She mentioned Rhode Island."

"That-a nice. You and-a Denise have a good time. I want-a meet her soon."

"Okay Ma. You will."

"Don't-a forget, call me. Ciao Bello."

"I love you Ma. Bella Mama."

Since my father passed away a year or so ago, my grandfather Guarino, now eighty-six, has moved into my mother's small Cape Cod style house in Harrison, NY. My mom, Inez, now in her mid sixties, still works at the Italian-American grocery store in the neighborhood. She's fluent in Italian, so it's easy for her to communicate with the Italian immigrants that live in the area. When she does speak English, as you heard, it's broken, but that doesn't diminish her innate intelligence. Now, she only wears black. I guess it's an Italian thing. When your husband passes away, the widow traditionally wears black. Mama is five feet two inches tall, dark eyes, and has graying black hair.

Denise walked out of the bathroom and into the bedroom, when the phone rang again. It was my brother Rich. "Hey Reynard, what's doin?

How are the boys?" I gave Richie the nick name Reynard after the cartoon character *Reynard the Fox*. Richie, like the cartoon character, is sly like a fox. You'd have to get up very early in the morning to put one

42

past him. He's thirty, five years younger than me, and everyone says he looks like Matt Damon. He and his wife Barbara have three kids. Matthew is nine, Jeffrey is eight, and Gregory is six. My family has been blessed with good looks. All my aunts, uncles, and cousins are *simpatico* to look at. My cousin Faith was crowned Miss Westchester in 2000.

Richie sounded upbeat. "Hey brother, everyone's fine. I haven't heard from you other than what I read in the newspapers. When are we going to meet Denise? By the way, it's your thirty-fifth birthday soon. Do you have any plans?"

"No plans. I just got off the phone with Ma. You sound just like her. She says I don't call. You know, she has a way of making you feel guilty."

"Yeah, I know." I said chuckling.

"So how's everything at the task force?"

He replied sighing heavily. "Oh, it's a long story."

"Um, what's going on?"

"I had a run in with the chief, and he's transferring me out of the accounting unit and into narcotics."

"Whoa, you've got to be fucking kidding me! No shit! What did you do?"

"The shit hit the fan when I told him to go fuck himself."

"What do you mean, you told him to go fuck himself? Rich, what do you got, a fucking death wish?"

"I'm not worried, I'll be assigned back. There's only a handful of forensic accountants. I happen to be the most senior and the most experienced."

"You know, you've got some set of balls. I'll say that much for you."

"Yeah, yeah, yeah. What about you? After the Larson and Daniels thing, what's up with you? "

I wasn't sure if Richie had heard about the Capolla murder and apparently he hadn't. I filled him in. I'd told him that I'd be going undercover driving one of Gary Corso's garbage trucks to try to find out who murdered Capolla and who attempted to take out Gary.

My brother's voice took a serious tone. "So, you're back at it. You need to be careful Frankie. This ain't no game. These fucking people play for keeps."

I tried to change the subject, and keep the conversation upbeat. "I'll be careful bro. Don't ya worry, they gotta worry about me. Just so you're not in the dark, I'm taking some days off before I start driving. Denise knows of a nice hotel in Providence. We're going to hang out there for a few days."

"Oh yeah! Good for you brother. I guess you'll be celebrating your birthday in Providence."

"It looks that way."

"Ah, well, have a nice time, and relax. Please tell Denise I said hi, and that Barbara and I can't wait to meet her. Have a happy birthday."

Laughing, I gave him a slight jab and said, "And don't forget to call Mom. And, by the way, she wants to meet Denise too."

Denise walked out of the bedroom and into the hallway wearing her black jogging suit. She grabbed me by the hand, tugging me into the living room, giving me a gentle nudge onto to the love seat. "Frankie I'm so excited. I just reserved a room at the Renaissance Providence Hotel. We can play tourists for a few days."

"Darling, I'm looking forward to it. A vacation will be good for both of us."

Denise jumped up and ran into the dining room, turning on the wall mounted radio. She kept the volume low, but we could hear the music as it filtered throughout the apartment. There was a gleam in her eye, as she walked back into the living room, plopping down next to me on the love seat. She was unable to contain her excitement. "Frankie this is our first vacation together. I'm so happy." She leaned in, kissing me on the cheek. Beyonce's, *Crazy in Love,* was playing in the background.

I was just as excited as she was. "I'm happy too, babe. I've never been to Providence. It'll be fun." Come to think of it, I've not been to too many places yet. Finances, family and job obligations have prevented that kind of freedom for me.

She stood, mumbling something I didn't understand, and with a sigh said, "Oh, I've got to find things to wear. I've got to get ready."

I'm thinking, I don't have much to pack. I'll have to make do with what I got.

I could have relaxed on the couch, but I forced myself up. Denise was mumbling to herself, apparently lost in the moment of picking out a few outfits to take. She was singing along to Alicia Keyes, *If I Ain't Got You.* I picked up the vibe and began to move to the rhythm of the music. I took hold of her and we began to dance. She laughed as I let go of her as she spun towards the bed and continued to pack. I didn't know if Denise was hungry, but I was. "Hun, it's getting late and we didn't have dinner yet. What did ya have in mind?"

As she threw some sexy lingerie into her bag she replied, "Let's order a kitchen sink pizza, besides, we should get to bed."

"Hey, that sounds good."

"What the pizza or bed?" she said giggling.

I winked, "Both."

She paused, and looked at me as if trying to remember in detail. "Oh, and by the way, I showed your picture to a couple of my girlfriends at work, and they think that you're very handsome. My friend Valarie said that you look like Johnny Depp."

I replied with a slight smile, "Oh she did? I'll take it. He happens to be one of my favorite actors."

She folded a white eyelet summer dress and seemed to slip away in thought and said, "Now you better start to pick out some clothes to take, and I'll order a pizza."

We ate in the living room and shared a bottle of Pinot Noir. Pinot Noir may be the toughest grape to grow, but the effort is worth it. It's the "Every Man's Grape." Denise and I shared a taste for it. We favored anything from the Russian River Valley in California. Perhaps that's another reason why we get along so well together.

Denise set the alarm for 8:00 A.M. to get an early start. It seemed that I'd just closed my eyes when the alarm went off. Rolling over towards Denise, I gently nudged her, "Its eight o'clock. A good time to get started."

Groggy, half asleep, her head buried under her pillow, and with a muffled voice said, "Oh, ok, just give me five minutes."

I pushed myself up, and sat on the side of the bed. Sitting there for a minute, I finally shook the sleep out of my eyes and headed for the bathroom. While showering, I thought of the ride up to Providence. Finally, I felt a sense of normalcy in my life, for the first time since my divorce. After all, splitting up a marriage is a strain, especially when you're the one who has to live alone. My thoughts drifted, thinking about driving the sanitation truck, and what unforeseen things might pop up. After all, I know nothing about that business and frankly, I'm apprehensive about driving a thirteen ton truck, and who wouldn't be?

Denise brought me back to earth when she shouted from the other side of the door, "Hey Frankie, I need to get into the shower too. Your breakfast is on the counter. Let's get going."

I shouted back, "C'mon in. I'll wash your back."

She opened the door, and stuck her head in. "Come on Frankie, I want to get going."

As I tilted my head up into the shower head, letting the warm water wash down onto my face I mumbled, "Okay, I'll be right out."

I grabbed one of the towels hanging on the rack, dried off, wrapped it around my waist, quickly brushed my teeth, and walked out. Denise gave me a peck on the cheek as she pushed passed. I thought to myself, God the girl is beautiful. She's really has turned my life around. I only hope she can put up with the long hours, and my time away from her.

I quickly threw on a fresh pair of jeans, a white linen shirt and walked into the kitchen. Denise had made coffee and poured me a bowl of Grape Nuts topped with blueberries. They were sitting on the countertop along with a pitcher of cream and bowl of sugar. I poured myself a cup of coffee. It was strong and black, the way I like it. Just as I was digging into the Grape Nuts, Denise walked in.

She was dressed in jeans and a yellow cardigan top. She wasn't wearing make up and didn't need any. She poured a cup of coffee and called me, as she walked into the dining room. "Frankie, you shouldn't be eating standing up, "C'mon into the dining room. Bring the coffee and cereal with you."

Sitting at the dining room table, we talked about our need for time away from our fast paced life. As we spoke, I couldn't help notice the sunlight bouncing off her light green eyes as it passed through the window. Denise leaned on her elbow, her hand supporting her head and said with a slight grin, "Frankie, I hope I made the coffee strong enough?"

I took a hefty swig of coffee and put the cup down. "It is perfect. Thank you. I'll bring the bags down to the car. Do you have the directions, and the hotel information?"

She nodded yes as she stood, planted a kiss on my cheek, and hurried to get her aviator sun glasses and purse. She scurried into the hallway yelling out, "C'mon Frankie, you said you'd bring the luggage down to the car."

We made our way down to the parking lot where I put the suitcases into Denise's champagne colored 2000 Chrysler Sebring convertible. It was a warm day in June, so we decided to put the top down for the drive to Providence. She wanted to drive and that was fine with me because I could sit back, relax and check out the scenery. We were staying at the Renaissance Providence Hotel in Federal Hill. The hotel is an historic building, built in 1750, and has recently been restored with all the modern amenities. It is centrally located within the city. The area is best known for its Italian-American community, abundant with fine Italian restaurants. I've never been to Providence, but as a history buff, I know that it has played an important role in American history during the American Revolution.

The trip took about three hours, driving north on Interstate 95 into Rhode Island. We talked, laughed, and listened to music as the warm spring breeze brushed passed our faces. Denise got off of I-95 at exit at 22C and drove about three miles into Providence.

We arrived at the hotel just in time to check in. A bell boy took our luggage and showed us to room 415, on the fourth floor. The room was simple. It was wall papered in soft yellow and blue stripes, with planked flooring. Naturally, it was decorated with an Early American style four-poster king size bed. The room was charming and over looked the Avenue of the Arts.

Denise looked the room over for a minute, grinning from ear to ear. "Frankie, don't you love it!"

"I love it, but I love you more, come here, baby."

She looked at me as if to say, *is sex the only thing on your mind.* "Honey, we'll have plenty of time for that. I want to explore Federal Hill. I think it will be fun to walk around the hill and see all the neat shops and restaurants."

I winked at her with a subtle grin and said, "Okay, I'll be ready in a minute, and we'll get directions from the concierge."

She turned towards me with an unforgettable smile. "I love you."

I looked back at her, and said, "I love you, too."

We took the elevator to the lobby, and spoke with the concierge. He gave us a map of Federal Hill and suggested that we see the Pinecone Arch, the gateway arch over Atwells Avenue. He told us not to miss the La Pigna sculpture, a pinecone, a traditional symbol of welcome, abundance, and quality. It hangs from the center of the arch. Atwells Avenue is within walking distance and most of the points of interest are on or just off the avenue. We headed for the arches and continued down Atwells Avenue, visiting trendy shops and Federalist homes. We must have walked for hours. We finally stopped at an outdoor café in DePasquale Square and sipped espresso coffee while noshing on Italian biscotti. The area reminded me of Arthur Avenue, an Italian-American enclave in the Bronx. We were having such a good time we didn't look at the time. It was already 6:00 P.M. and we didn't have dinner reservations. I asked the waiter to suggest a good Italian restaurant in the area. He recommended Anna Maria's, just up the street. He gave me the number and I made a reservation for eight o'clock. I paid the check and we found our way back to the hotel.

It was about 7:00 P.M. when we arrived back in the room. Denise practically ripped my clothes off and said playfully, "Let's get into the shower, hon." She didn't have to tell me twice. Before her clothes hit the floor, I was aroused. She stood there with a come hither look as we walked into the bathroom and into the shower. I spun her around into my arms, pressing my body into hers. We were both overwhelmed with passion.

The warmth of the water falling on our heated bodies engaged us completely in the moment. I poured liquid soap into my hands and began to gently massage her. She pulled me close, kissing me passionately, as we made love in rhythmical sync. Groaning wildly, she let out a scream, "Frankie, love me. Hold me." She moaned into my ear, "I love the way you love me." We then held each other, basking in the afterglow of our love making. We could barely walk. We wrapped towels around ourselves and walked into the living room. Denise revealing a lusty laugh, smiled and said, "We better get dressed for dinner."

As I was about to put on my jeans, my cell phone rang. It was Friedman. "Frank, it's Zack."

I couldn't believe that he was calling me on my day off. I thought what now?

"Hey Zack, what's up?"

"I hope that you're sitting down Frankie because I have some shocking news. Gary Corso was shot to death early this morning."

I sat on the bed trying to fathom what he just said. "What?"

"Sometime before 6:00 A.M. this morning, he and unidentified woman were shot to death while sitting in his car. They were parked in the carting company yard."

I jumped up from the bed, and paced around the room. "Are you fucking kidding me?"

Zack, in a rushed voice, said, "Look, I've got to go. I'll fill you in when I see you. Howell told me you took a couple of days off."

"Yeah, I'm in Providence, but I can come back."

"Right now, it's not necessary. I'll have more information in a day or so. The New Rochelle P.D. is trying to come up with leads. They're talking to his wife."

"Are you sure you don't want me to come down?"

"Yes, I'm sure. I'll be in touch."

I needed to sit and digest what had just happened. I sat back down on the bed, thinking that Gary was alive just a short while ago and now he's dead. Denise had a puzzled look, as she stood in the middle of the room wrapped in a towel. "Frankie, what was that all about? What's going on?"

The color left my face. "My new assignment, I mean, the guy I'm supposed to be working for just got shot to death."

Denise stood there shaking her head, trying to make sense of what I just said. "Someone was murdered?"

"Yes. He was shot dead this morning."

I could tell from the look on her face that she was trying to understand the world I lived in. I wrestled with the thought of meeting Gary the other day and just now hearing he's dead.

Denise ran over and hugged me. "I hope I can be strong enough for you Frank. I know that Helen wasn't."

Holding onto her, I thought about the breakup of my marriage and wondered if Denise was strong enough to handle the life I'm in. I didn't say anything, but in my heart, I hoped that she would be. I loved her very much. I gazed at her and said, "Honey, we should get dressed now and start heading to the restaurant."

Just then, Chief Howell called. He sounded anxious. He repeated what Zack had just told me. "Frank, the body count is climbing, and the DA wants an arrest yesterday. He knows that it's gonna take some time, but he's eager."

Howell could turn on a New York minute, so I was careful how I couched things. "Chief, just how many detectives are assigned to the investigation besides the two from New Rochelle?"

"Besides you, that's it."

"Look chief, I'm only one guy. We need more manpower. Are there any leads on the Capolla homicide?"

In an irritable voice he replied, "No. No leads."

"Chief, I'm not telling you anything you don't know, but every informant we have needs to be squeezed for information. These murders have organized crime written all over them."

For once, Howell, the characteristic bully, remained calm. "Well Frank, Hogan is counting on you and so am I. Dana Corso will be running the business alone. You'll be meeting with her as soon as you get back. Understand?"

"Fine, so who was with him when he was killed?"

"A female, but right now we're still trying to identify her. I'll text you Dana's phone number. She's expecting to hear from you Sunday night. Make sure you call her."

It was almost eight o'clock, and we had to get a move on. The romantic atmosphere had certainly changed since my last two phone calls. We dressed in relative silence and decided to walk to the restaurant instead of driving. In hindsight, that decision turned out to be the right one. We walked through the hotel lobby and I noticed a few hotel guests turned their heads as we passed. I guess we made a handsome couple. Denise was just over six feet tall when she put her stilettos on. Her short white skirt and Hermes belt blended nicely with her white cotton blouse revealing every natural curve in her well proportioned body. Besides jeans, I wore a blue collared shirt, and a dark blue Ralph Lauren sport jacket. It was the only sport jacket I owned.

We walked a few blocks to the restaurant. We were greeted by a starchy looking character, dressed in a tuxedo, in his mid-fifties. He asked if we had reservations. "Yes," I replied, "They're under the name MacKenzie."

He glanced for a second at the booking register and with a forced smile said, "Right this way."

He escorted us to our booth and seated us. The booths line a glass partition wall, separating the room from the hallway. White damask table clothes adorned each table and small crystal vases holding yellow roses were centered on top. There's a full size mahogany bar off the dining room. The place really had a European feel to it. A short time later a very perky waitress came over to take our drink order. Denise ordered a Chardonnay and I ordered a Campari and soda with a twist of lemon. The waitress asked if we wanted a bottle of sparkling water to start.

I replied, "Sparkling water would be great."

"I'll be right back with your drinks."

The ambiance of the restaurant brought us back to the romantic place we were in before the upsetting phone calls. We sat there for a moment enjoying each others company making small talk. Denise decided to have the scungilli salad appetizer and soft shell crabs sautéed in a white wine butter sauce with capers for her entree. I went with the prosciutto and honeydew melon appetizer and the braised veal chop. We ordered a bottle of Chardonnay to go with the meal.

Denise reached across the table and took hold of my hand looking starry-eyed. "I really love the atmosphere here. Don't you?

I replied softly. "It's wonderful when I'm with you and sharing moments like this."

The waitress returned with our appetizers and placed them in front of us, and asked if everything was okay. Denise shook her head yes and said, "Everything is just wonderful. Thank you."

If the appetizers were any indication of what was to come, we were in for a real treat. No sooner than we finished our first glass of wine, our entrees arrived. We devoured them. After enjoying our meal and finishing the bottle of wine, Denise noticed two men on the other side of the room staring at me. At first she didn't say anything, but when they continued to stare, she mentioned it. "Frankie, there are two guys sitting over there, staring at you."

I looked cross the room, really not expecting to see anyone I knew. Turning to Denise I replied, "What two guys?"

Denise cocked her head toward two men and asked if I knew them. I looked at them, but I didn't recognize them. "No, I don't know them. Maybe I look like someone they know." They continued staring, while they spoke to one another.

Clearly their stares were upsetting Denise and making me feel uneasy. I stared back at them. One of the men suddenly stood up, looked directly at me, and started to approach our table. I was trying to place him, but I couldn't. I reached down to my waist and placed my hand on my 9mm. The guy was nicely dressed, definitely an Italian-American, with dark black hair. She sat there, staring up at this guy, who was now standing over us. I didn't know what to make of the situation.

"Frankie, you don't recognize me. Do you?" he said.

I stiffened up. My hand was firm on the butt of my gun. "No, I don't know who you are."

Denise was now fidgeting with her table napkin. She looked anxious. "Frankie, do you know him?"

Clearly annoyed I replied, "No. I don't know him." I stood up, looking directly into his eyes, and said, "Who are you?"

He replied sarcastically, "I know you don't remember me, but I'm Nick Galgano's nephew, Joey. You put me in jail a while back. I came over to say hello. And by the way, I own this restaurant; enjoy your dinner."

I didn't know what to say. I stared back at him. I trailed off for a second, remembering him. It was Joey Galgano. I used to pick up his numbers work. I paused briefly. "Yeah, Joey. Now I remember you. You've put on a little weight, and grew a beard."

He continued, as if he wanted to get it off his chest. "You ran one of my uncle's numbers spots on a Hundred and Fifty Third Street in the South Bronx, but you turned out to be a cop and put a lot of us away."

I raised my voice, "Yeah, what of it!"

He grinned and said, "I just wanted to say hello." He then offered me his hand but I didn't take it. He turned with a sneer, and walked back to his table.

I quickly motioned to the waitress for the check. She ran over and said that Mr. Galgano has picked up the check. I told her thanks, but no thanks, digging out one hundred and fifty dollars from my wallet, telling her to keep the change. "Let's go honey."

We walked out. I could feel Joe Galgano's eyes at the back of my head. I took Denise's arm and looked around to see if someone was waiting outside. We quickly started to walk back to the hotel. I remember that night like it was yesterday. The night sky was clear and there were thousands of stars lighting the sky. The air was warm. Denise held my arm so tightly that I had to loosen her grip. Her eyes were as wide as silver dollars. "Frankie, I'm scared, what just happened in there? Are we going to be okay?"

I was trying my best to calm her. My head whirled around a few times to see if we were being followed. We weren't. I said calmly, "We're fine. Nothing to worry about." She didn't say anything, she didn't have to. The girl was scared to death. I kept looking back, my hand on my gun, to see if anyone was behind us. I didn't see anyone.

"Frankie, please take me home."

"Let's not let this spoil our trip. There's nothing to worry about."

She rolled her eyes. "Frankie, I'm not used to the world you live in. I don't know if I'll ever get used to it. I want to leave first thing in the morning."

We left the hotel early Sunday morning. On the ride back to Bronxville, we hardly spoke.

CHAPTER SIX

Friedman had called me on Sunday and said that we were meeting with Dana Corso at her home later that evening. It was decided that I'd pick him up at 8:30 P.M. at his apartment in New Rochelle. Zack was standing in front of his building when I pulled up. As he got into the car he gave me a friendly hello. It's a twenty-minute ride to the Corso house and we had a lengthy conversation on the way to Scarsdale about the murders of Gary and the female who was later identified as Clare Iverson, rumored to be his girlfriend. He said that after Gary had been shot the first time in the Bronx, he began to carry an unlicensed .38 caliber pistol. New Rochelle Detectives Straub and Barry who are investigating the Capolla homicide, decided to pay him a visit at the yard after they initially interviewed him. They noticed the butt of the gun sticking out of his pants pocket and asked to see his pistol permit. He didn't have one. When questioned about the gun, he told them that he bought it on the street, to protect himself. Thinking that Gary knew more than he was telling about the Capolla homicide, they decided to arrest him on the spot. He was charged with felony possession of an illegal firearm. They figured the arrest would pressure him to give up what he knew about the Capolla murder. They were wrong. Gary told them that he knew nothing about the murder and a few days later, he was shot to death.

I looked over at Zack, shaking my head in disgust. "You gotta be kidding me. If those morons didn't take the fucking gun away from him he might have had a chance."

"Ya, maybe he would have had a chance. But those two detectives are hardcore. All they cared about was closing the Capolla homicide."

I muttered something and said, "How those cowboys can sleep at night is beyond me."

By the tone of his voice, Zack was upset too. "I don't know Frankie. But apparently they can."

Zack continued, "Gary and Clare Iverson must have been meeting in his office. After their tryst, Gary was about to drive out of his New Rochelle yard when they were shot multiple times in the head with a small caliber pistol. They were both found slumped over in the front seat of his Mercedes, the engine still running. Right now we don't know if there was more than one shooter. The same small caliber rounds that were used in the Capolla homicide killed Gary and the girl. It's the same shooter. Detectives found a twelve-gauge shotgun in the back seat, but Gary didn't get a chance to use it. There was no forensic evidence found at the scene. Sadly, Clare's autopsy indicated that she was pregnant."

I was unconsciously tugging on my mustache.

Zack glanced over at me. He was tapping his fingers on the arm rest, because I was annoying him. "Hey Frankie you're all wound up, and for Christ sake keep your eyes on the road. And stop fiddling with your mustache, you're driving me crazy."

I shot back at Zack unable to contain my anxiety. "Zack, these killings gotta be Mafia hits. I'll be a sitting duck in that truck if they find out that I'm a cop."

"Look, you'll be fine. You know how to take care of yourself."

I sat straight up in the seat. My body stiffened as I raised my voice, "Fucking easy for you to say."

Zack gave me a hard stare and didn't say anything. I asked him how Gary knew the Iverson woman. "We haven't been able to connect the dots yet. All we know is that she was a showgirl who danced at the Mandalay Bay Hotel in Vegas."

I wondered if Dana knew that Gary had a girlfriend. Maybe her motive for wanting him dead was two fold. One, she found out that he was having an affair with Clare Iverson, and two, she killed him to collect on his life insurance policy.

I asked Zack, "Do we know the payout on Gary's life insurance policy?"

Zack flashed a smile and replied, "She gets a cool three million."

I shrugged my shoulders. "Wow, is that right? Maybe she had him killed for the money? Maybe she found out about Clare Iverson? You know what they say about a woman scorned."

I turned off Wilmot Road onto Saxon Woods Road, driving into the Corso's long driveway leading up to a mansion. As we pulled up in front of the house, I leaned over towards Zack and nudged him. "Look Zack, you and I know that Clare Iverson happened to be in the wrong place at the wrong time. It got her killed." He nodded his head yes and said, "It's a damn shame."

The Corso house is magnificent. It must be ten thousand square feet, constructed of white clapboard, with black shutters. It looked more like the White House than a private home in Scarsdale. It sat on two manicured acres surrounded by Elm, White Birch, and Magnolia trees that gave a certain elegance to the landscape. It just goes to show how much money there is in garbage.

We got out of the car, just about to walk up two sets of slate steps when Dana Corso opened the front door, holding a martini. She was dressed in a black sweater, buttoned at the neck, and black skintight spandex pants. She wasn't wearing much make-up, and frankly she didn't need it. Dana extended her hand, and after short pleasantries, we followed her into the banquet room. Although the room was dimly lit, I noticed a fresco painted on the ceiling. It was a replica of God creating the world that was painted on the ceiling of the Sistine Chapel by Michelangelo. Zack asked about a few of her paintings. She stopped, pointing to one of the paintings and said, "It's an original portrait painted by Giovanni Bellini, a master painter of the fifteenth century."

She raised the light on a large crystal chandelier hanging over a fifteen foot hand carved walnut table. Gesturing with her hand, she said, "Please have a seat." There was bottled water, a bottle of Grey Goose vodka, a decanter of martini's and glasses on the table. She sat down at the head of the table and said with a forced smile, "Would you care for a drink?"

Zack took a seat on one side of Dana, and poured himself a glass of water, while I sat on the other side of her, directly across the table from Zack. Dana picked up her martini and took a hefty swig. We looked at one another perplexed. It was apparent that she'd been drowning her sorrows in booze.

Friedman, the gentleman that he is, began with an air of sadness, "Dana, you have our deepest sympathy for the loss of your husband."

She looked at Zack, as her eyes began to well up. "Thank you, Mr. Friedman. May I call you Zack?" She lowered her head, staring down at the table and burst into tears.

Zack's tone took a serious turn. "Certainly you may, however, it's important that Detective Santorsola understands what he's getting into. We have a few questions."

She tried to compose herself, but the tears kept coming.

Zack attempted to calm her, and said softly clearing his throat. "Mrs. Corso, we know how difficult this must be for you, but we can't postpone these questions any longer."

She nodded yes, wiping her tears from her cheeks with a handkerchief. She was intoxicated. Slurring her words she replied, "Please call me Dana."

Zack leaned towards Dana and said, "Dana we feel very strongly that your husband's murder is an attempt to force you out of business."

Dana paused for a moment thumbing the corners of her handkerchief. "Yes, I know you do. My father-in-law Carmine, offered to buy it back as a gesture of kindness. He feels it's too much for me to handle."

I interrupted, "Tell me about your relationship with your father-in-law."

"Well, it was strained. Gary….."

"Go on." I said.

She poured another martini from the decanter in front of her. Her eyes were red, and it seemed like she was having a hard time getting her thoughts together. Pausing for a second, she looked at me and said, "Between Carmine's gumares and his gambling, there was no time for anyone or anything else. Gary argued with his father about the situation. Gary and his father had a love-hate relationship. All Carmine cares about is money, and his so called family."

"What do you mean his so called family?" Friedman asked.

"You know exactly what I mean. The Mafia family he took an oath to live and die by consumed him. I'm sure you know all about the illegal things he's involved in."

Friedman was on a roll, taking full advantage of her drunkenness. Dana spoke like she was in a confessional. "Dana, you're right. I know what he's alleged to be involved in, but I want to hear it from you."

"I know he made a lot of money from illegal gambling and loan sharking." He's had many girlfriends over the years. That's why Gary's mother Connie is so miserable. My mother-in-law has put up with his shit for years. Carmine has had girlfriend after girlfriend. He has made a mockery of their marriage. She can't divorce him, he'd kill her. My husband was following in his father's filthy, unfaithful footsteps."

I asked, "Dana, what'd you tell Carmine when he said he'd buy the business back?"

She slurred the words, "I told him that I didn't want to sell it. Gary would want me to keep it."

"What'd he say?"

She hesitated for a second, "Uh, he".....She paused in mid-sentence thinking about what Carmine said. "He said that he was going to find out who killed his son, and deal with it his own way."

Zack tensed up in the chair, and said emphatically, "Your father-in-law can't know that Frank is working for you. We don't want Frank to get hurt."

Dana looked over at me, softening her refined facial features. "Of course not. I certainly don't want Frank to get hurt."

I asked abruptly. "Dana, do you know who killed your husband?"

Without an ounce of emotion in her voice, she replied, "No. No I don't."

I poured a glass of water and took a sip, glancing at Zack, and back to Dana and asked, "Dana, tell me what you know about Clare Iverson."

"I don't know anything about her. Gary's cheated on me in the past, but in the last few months our relationship has been rapidly deteriorating. Right before he was killed, he told me wanted a divorce. He said he was in love with someone else, and was going to marry her. I didn't want a divorce. I tried to save my marriage. I've loved that man since I was sixteen years old. He was my life. But, I knew this time it was over. Clare Iverson put an end to it. What did she have that I don't have? She couldn't have loved him like I do." Dana lowered her head, sobbing.

Zack and I took a hard look at one another. This was as good a time as any to ask. I asked, "Dana, Dana, look at me. Did you have anything to do with Gary or Clare's death?"

Dana lifted her head weeping. She shouted, "No Frank! I had nothing to do with their deaths. Nothing!"

My eyes were centered on Dana's eyes. "Okay Dana. We needed to ask that question. Please try to calm yourself." She tried to regain her composure.

Zack asked, after a short pause, "So Dana, tell us about the garbage business. How many trucks do you own?"

She replied, again slurring her words, "I have five trucks. Frank will be driving the truck that Lou Vitullo drove. He left the company when they began assaulting the drivers. A driver was beaten up yesterday."

Zack raised his eyebrows and asked, "So, are the drivers still being assaulted?"

She shook her head yes. "Yes, they are. I can't afford to lose another driver."

Making direct eye contact with Dana, I asked, "Dana, what can I expect on my first day?"

Dana, hardly able to speak, said that I'd be given a galley, a list of the sixty or so commercial customers in Rye and Port Chester that are scheduled to have their containers emptied twice a week, Monday through Friday. Nutsey Fuganza will work the hopper on the truck.

I asked about the other communities that her company serviced.

She said, "We have contracts in Southern Westchester and the North Bronx. The drivers have been with us ever since Gary bought the business from his father three years ago."

She told me that her office manager, Jimmy Newcomb, handles the payroll and general administration of the company. Dana said that Newcomb is her right hand man. His nickname is Shorty. I chuckled to myself, Nutsey Fuganza, now Shorty. I wondered who I'd meet next. I gave Dana my cell phone number, and asked her if my fictitious statistics had been added to her list of employees. She said, "Yes, Gary put together an employee folder.......before......he..." She broke down, sobbing uncontrollably.

"Dana I'm so sorry, but please, if Newcomb asks, I was hired by Gary after Vitullo quit. And, when you see me in the yard, treat me like the rest of the drivers."

Her voice labored, she replied, "Certainly, you're just another employee."

Zack looked at his watch. "Look, it's getting late. Frank will be starting in a few hours. I think its best we leave."

We pushed away from the table and stood. Dana extended her hand first to Zack and then to me. Inches away from my face she said in a whisper, "Your secret is safe with me."

I didn't say anything for a moment. "Dana, I hope so."

She sighed, "Frank, what I want is for you to find the killer of my husband."

Dana then walked us to the front door, and waited for us to get into our car before shutting it.

CHAPTER SEVEN

The alarm clock sounded at 1:45 A.M., waking me and Denise. Denise rolled over muttering incoherently. "Frankie, are you okay? What time is it?"

Still asleep, I forced myself up, sitting on the edge of the bed. Stretching my neck muscles I began to roll my head around my shoulders trying to wake up. I guess I was thinking out loud mumbling, "Oh my God. It's a quarter to two in the morning." I slowly got up, leaned over, and gave her a playful pat on her rump, as she lay there half asleep.

Before falling back to sleep, in a muffled voice she said, "I love you. Please be careful."

I then stumbled into the bathroom to dress quietly. I thought about taking my sawed off shotgun, but it was hard for me to conceal. I began keeping a shotgun under my front seat several years ago, after a friend of mine was killed by a maniac during a routine traffic stop on the Bronx River Parkway. People might think that what I do for a living is dangerous, but I think that highway cops have the most dangerous job of all. They never know who they're stopping. In my friend Carl's case, he stopped a guy for speeding who was wanted for a double homicide in Virginia. That stop, unfortunately, cost him his life.

Before walking out, I took a quick look around, shut the lights, closed the door behind me, and down the five flights of stairs to the street. My car was parked in the rear of the building. It's so quiet in the early morning hours, and I was thinking of how much I loved the calm. In a few short minutes, my peace would end and I'd be experiencing the harshness of the day.

It's only a twenty-minute drive to Corso's yard from my apartment. When I got there, the gate was open. It was 3:05 A.M. I parked behind an old beat up Ford Mustang parked on the side of a two story redbrick building. Several men were in the yard milling around and talking. I guess they were unwinding before jumping into their trucks and heading out on their garbage routes. I stepped out of the Cadillac and walked over to the first guy I saw. He was about to pull himself up into the cab of his truck as I introduced myself. "Hey, I'm Frank Miranda. I start today. Where's the boss?"

He smiled and said in a rough tone, "Second floor. I'm Dave. Jimmy is waiting for you in the office." He got into the cab, closing the door. He looked out of the driver's side window and said, "Good luck, Miranda."

There was a set of wrought iron stairs leading up to the office. One of the trucks rolled out of the yard as I climbed the stairs. It was showtime. I felt like an athlete waiting for the whistle to start the game. My heart was racing. I was apprehensive about meeting Jimmy. I knocked on the steel framed door and walked in. Jimmy Newcomb was standing with his back to a battered wooden desk. When he saw me, his light blue eyes seemed to burrow through me. Dana was right. He's only about 5 feet tall. I noticed that his long light brown hair was tangled and matted. He wore a white sweatshirt covered by blue denim coveralls, and brown work boots. The pug faced little bastard looked like he ate nails for breakfast. There were a number of framed pictures of Gary and his wife placed on the desk, along with a glass ashtray filled with burned out cigarette and cigar butts. Across the office I noticed a guy who looked like an unmade bed, seated on a weathered black leather sofa.

Newcomb's eyes widened as he moved towards me clenching his fists, shouting, "You're fuckin late! You're supposed to show up at three! Not three fifteen!"

I stood there staring at him for split second thinking, should I really piss the free-hole off and see what he's made of, or let it go? I figured what the hell. I looked at my watch, and then back at Newcomb smirking, "It's only three ten."

Newcomb's jaw dropped and blood rushed to his face. I glanced over at the guy on the sofa. He was squirming in his pants, and looked like he wanted to be somewhere else. Newcomb was fuming. In a threatening tone, he said, "We start at three. You got that Miranda, or whatever your fucking name is!"

Frank Santorsola

I wanted to knock the little cocksucker out of his boots, but instead I took a deep breath, calming myself. "Uh, sure Jimmy. I'll be here at three from now on. Sorry."

In his high pitched voice, the little bastard yelled, "Only my fucking friends call me by my first name! You're not my friend. Got it?"

My blood was boiling over. I started for him, but I stopped myself. He noticed, and it incensed him more. "Yeah, Mr. Newcomb, I got it."

He continued shouting, pointing to the guy on the sofa, "This is your hopper guy, Nutsey Fuganza. He'll show you the ropes!"

I looked over at Nutsey, and noticed his forearms. They were like tree trunks, and I shit you not, he looked just like Popeye. He couldn't have been any older than forty. He was slightly balding, barrel-chested, with brown stringy hair, tied back in a ponytail. A skullcap sat on his lap. The only thing that Nutsey needed was a corn cob pipe, and a girlfriend named Olive Oil.

Newcomb hobbled back behind the desk, sat in a large leather swivel chair, lit a cigar, and blew the smoke across the desk into my face. Leaning back in the chair, he asked sharply, "Where did you haul garbage before?"

"I picked up garbage when I was stationed at Fort Bragg."

He rolled the cigar over to one side of his mouth, removing a manila folder from a desk drawer. Thumbing through it, he asked, "So Gary hired you. How did you know Gary?"

"I met him at the Eastchester Diner. He sat next to me at the counter. We struck up a friendly conversation and I mentioned I was looking for work. It's too bad he's dead."

Leaning back in the chair he nodded in agreement. "Yes, it is. He was a good guy." He paused for a few seconds, as if in thought, took another long drag on the cigar, again blowing the smoke in my face. Newcomb, trying to get a gauge on me, asked, "So what kind of work did you do before running into Gary? It doesn't say here."

I replied matter-of-factly, "I owned a small landscaping business in Connecticut, but that didn't work out. A larger company undercut me and stole my customers."

Just then the desk phone rang. Jimmy quickly picked it up. The conversation was short. "Yes, he is Dana, he's here. Huh, okay fine." And he hung up.

My mind was racing. I couldn't wait to talk to Nulligan. I wanted him to run a criminal check on Newcomb.

Newcomb looked over at Nutsey, gesturing with his head as if it was time to go, then leaned forward and handed me the galley sheet for the weekly pick ups. He took a set of keys from the corner of the desk and threw them at me. He barked at Nutsey, "Show Miranda which truck to take. "Get going. And Nutsey, you'll be dumping at the Rye transfer station on Oakland Beach Avenue."

The truck was parked nose out in the garage. I looked over at my car thinking, that's where Gary and his girlfriend were probably murdered. We climbed in the cab of a thirteen ton, five speed standard shift Mack garbage truck. Thank God my father was old school and taught me how to drive his standard shift Chevy Impala. I remember how impatient my Dad was when I rear-ended a car when he was teaching me how to parallel park. At the time, I thought that he should have kept pace with the times and driven an automatic shift. But, he wanted me to drive a standard shift car. If it weren't for him, my undercover role would have been impossible.

Once in the truck, I got a closer look at Nutsey. He appeared to be a nervous sort of guy, constantly fidgeting with his skull cap. He looked over at me, gnawing on his bottom lip, I guess trying to figure me out. He grunted, "C'mon, start the fuckin truck. We gotta go, or Shorty will go through the roof. We got 20 stops, and at this rate it'll take us all day."

I thought, yeah it'll take us all day alright. When he finds out that I've never driven a garbage truck, he'll really get a case of the yips. I pushed the starter and the big diesel engine cranked over, purring like a kitten. I shifted into first gear, and slowly drove out of the yard onto Fourth Street. I looked over at Nutsey and asked, "Where to?"

Nutsey gazed back at me with a look like he didn't believe what he'd just heard. He was freaking out. "What da fuck you mean! Where to? Rye! Look at the fucking galley. The first stop is The Rye Pub. It's a 50 yarder."

I shrugged my shoulders then grabbed the wheel, turning it to the right. "Okay, take it easy Nutsey, we'll get there."

I headed to Interstate 95 North. I guess I was doing fine since Nutsey wasn't saying much. I nudged his arm. "Nutsey, I got a lot of questions."

His eyes were closed, as he rested his head on the passenger side window. "Oh, yeah, like what?"

"For one thing, what's up with Newcomb? He's a nasty little prick."

He opened his eyes, turning toward me yawning, "Stay away from him. He's got a mean streak. You got it?"

Intent on finding out all I could about Newcomb, I pressed Nutsey for more information. "They say his nickname is Shorty."

Nutsey paused for a split second, and then spat out, "You better never let him hear you call him that if you know what's good for you. He hates it."

I glared at him for a moment. "And, ah, what's he gonna do?"

He just sat there and stared out the window. I thought, gees, there must be a lot more to find out about Newcomb. He seems to hold a hammer over the guys. They're afraid of him.

It's not uncharacteristic for guys, especially wise guys to have nicknames. I was called Frankie "Cheech" Miranda. It was given to me by one of the guys in the organized crime crew that I infiltrated. Just so you understand, Cheech is slang in Italian for Frank. And speaking of nicknames, I was curious to find out how Louis Fuganza, a/ka/ Nutsey got his nickname, and there was no better time to ask him.

As I pulled into traffic on I-95 heading for Rye, I asked him bluntly. "So why do they call you Nutsey?"

Finally breaking a smile, he looked over grinning. "Nutsey, well, because I've done a lot of crazy things in my life."

"Like what?"

"For one, when I was twelve, I jumped off the Third Avenue Bridge into the Harlem River, in Manhattan." He leaned back again against the seat and began to laugh.

I couldn't believe what I was hearing. "Ya what, you jumped off the Third Avenue Bridge? Why?"

He paused again as if thinking about the reason he jumped off the bridge. He lit a cigarette, took a drag, and said, as he exhaled, "Well, we lived on 135th Street in East Harlem. It was a hot summer's day and I wanted to cool off, so I jumped into the Harlem River. The friends I was with started to call me Nutsey from then on."

I scratched my head and asked, "Is there anything else?"

"Yeah," he said laughing again, "When I was fifteen, we moved to the Bronx. Me and a couple of friends tied a guy to a tree in Bronx Park up on East 180th Street, put leaves and sticks around his feet and set him on fire."

I looked at him and shook my head in amazement. "What happened to him?"

"The Fire Department came and put out the fire."

"Was he okay?"

Nutsey's was now laughing. "Yeah, he was okay, but his shoes got singed."

Just the way he said it, I started to laugh. He speaks off the cuff and without any filters. The more he said, and how he said it, the harder I laughed. Now I know why they call him Nutsey. He's nuts. I was going to ask him if anyone ever told him that he looks like Popeye, but I decided not to go there.

Nutsey seemed to be relaxed as he puffed away on his cigarette. Naturally I was apprehensive about the whole situation and not paying attention to my driving, continually down shifting the truck into third gear.

Nutsey leaned over and began poking me with his forefinger shouting, "Stop down shifting."

I nodded okay and replied, "Sorry Nutsey. My mind is somewhere else."

As we neared the exit, I thought that I'd test the waters and see what he knew about Gary's murder. As the truck rumbled towards the Harrison exit I asked, "So Nutsey, why would someone want to kill Gary? He was a nice guy, Right? I heard that his partner was murdered, too."

I watched Nutsey's hands as they nervously rolled around each other. He took one long drag of his cigarette and flipped it out the window.

He cranked the window back up, and said in a somber tone, "I really don't want to talk about it. Drive." He pointed to the road sign for the Harrison and said, "Take the exit."

I turned off of I-95, into Rye. About a mile up the road, Nutsey pointed to Locust Avenue where I made a left, driving into the Rye Highlands. I turned down Delia Street, and saw The Rye Pub on the right, the name on a dark green sign with gold letters hanging over the front door. I let the truck idle. I figured that this was as good a time as any to break the news to Nutsey that I've never driven a garbage truck in my life, and knew nothing about picking up garbage. "Look Nutsey. I got a confession to make."

"Yeah, what is it?"

"Ya know, I really needed a job, so I lied about driving a garbage truck."

Nutsey's eyes lit up. "What? You say what?"

"I've never driven a garbage truck in my life."

He looked like he was about to shit his pants. His face turned the color of mud, and he looked like his circulatory system was shutting down. He screamed, "Whoa, what d' ya mean you never drove a garbage truck?"

"Nutsey, I had to lie. I needed a job. You can understand that."

Nutsey's mouth hung open, and his eyebrows almost reached his hair line.

I looked over, pleading, "Look, Nutsey, I need your help. You have to show me what to do or I'm fucked. I need this job."

Nutsey shook his head from side to side. "What'd I look like a garbage instructor?"

He sat there in silence, staring out the window shaking his head for a moment. Then, in a sympathetic tone he said, "Okay, okay, I'll help you, I got no choice. There's a 50-yard container to unload, and another nineteen stops to go. Let's get started."

I smiled and said, "Thanks Nutsey. You're a real stand up guy, I owe you."

He opened the cab door, stepping out onto the sidewalk and said, "Back the truck into the driveway. The dumpster is at the end of the driveway."

What a relief. Now I could begin to breathe easier. Looking down at Nutsey who was about to walk into the common driveway that separated the pub from another building, I barked, "Nutsey, I won't forget this."

Nutsey walked into the driveway shouting something that I didn't quite get. I yelled back. "What did you say?"

This time I heard him loud and clear. "Use your side view mirrors to back up to the container. I'll guide you. The pins on the rear of the truck slide into the sleeves on the container."

I pulled the truck across the street and began backing it into the driveway, using the rear view mirrors as a guide. I slowly inched my way back to the container. Nutsey was standing in front of the container motioning with his hand, waving me back. My head was sticking half out of the window, I asked, "Why doesn't this truck pick up the containers from the front, and dump them into the top of the truck like I've seen? It looks a lot easier."

Nutsey yelled back, "This is an old truck. Gary was about to replace it. When you hook up, I'll connect the cable to the container, and engage the winch." He pointed to a lever on the back of the truck. "The garbage will fall into the hopper and the hopper will push the garbage into the truck."

I was about ten feet from the container and shouted, "Nutsey how does the hopper work?"

"When you're hooked up, I'll show you." I could see him pointing to a twelve inch handle on the right side of the truck. "This lever operates the hopper." Nutsey continued to wave me back, shouting, "C'mon on back, C'mon on back."

I finally felt the truck bump the container and hoped that the pins had hit their mark. I looked back at Nutsey. "Nutsey, am I in?"

Shaking his head, no, he yelled, "No, pull up and try again."

I pulled up about five feet and then began to slowly back up, using the side view mirrors to guide me. I was sure that I was going to connect this time. Nutsey, standing off to the side was waving me back with his hand and yelling, "More to the right. That's good. Now straighten it out."

Again I felt the back of the truck hit the container and yelled, "Am I in now?"

"No!" he shouted. His face contorted by his frustration. I'm sure he was sorry that he was in this mess. With both hands on his hips, he looked down shaking his head, crying out, "C'mon, try it again."

Again, I took a deep breath and pulled the truck up, then backed it slowly to the container. This time I was positive that I'd succeed. But that wasn't the case. I sat there muttering a few curses, thinking, *how the fuck could this be possible? How many times could I miss hooking up to the container?* I gripped the steering wheel so tightly that my fucking knuckles turned white. I didn't think that it would be this tough. Frustrated almost to the point of firing a couple of shots into the air, I screamed, "Huh, you gotta be fucking kidding me? I'm not hooked up. I can't fucking believe it!"

Nutsey just stood there, irritated. I have to give the guy credit. He maintained his cool, calmly replying, "C'mon, try it again. You can do it."

I was nervous and frustrated, thinking that we have another twenty or so stops to make. We've been here for forty-five minutes already, and at this rate we won't be finished until midnight. If I don't pick up this stop soon, Jimmy will know that I'm a fake. I took a long breath to keep my heart from blowing through my chest. I hit the gas pedal a little too hard and the truck lurched forward about fifteen feet. Nutsey screamed, "What the fuck you doing?"

I didn't answer him. I was afraid of what I might do to him. I took another breath, trying to calm down, as I backed the truck up towards the container. This time, thank Christ; I could hear the pins engage the sleeves of the container. Nutsey was jumping up and down, and, shouting," You're in, you're in!"

I jumped out of the truck, looking like I'd just won a gold medal in the Olympic Games. Nutsey quickly hooked up the cable line to the eye hook on the top of the container. He slowly monitored the flow of garbage as it fell into the hopper. I studied Nutsey's every movement, so I'd know how to operate the truck. We jumped back into the truck and headed for the next stop.

Nutsey's hands were trembling as he lit another cigarette. He glanced over sighing, "Next stop is the Chase bank on Purchase Street. I hope this stop is quicker than the first."

As I drove into the parking lot, I saw the 10-yard container sitting up against the side of the bank. Nutsey, mumbled, "Its only paper." He jumped out of the truck and said, "Back up so we can hook up, and get out of here. It's getting late."

I pulled the truck in position. There were a number of people parking, and walking into the bank. It was 8:30 A.M. Nutsey gestured towards the container. I started back a little too fast and didn't see or hear Nutsey yelling for me to stop. It was too late. He stood there shrugging his shoulders, shaking his head in disbelief, as he watched me hit the container driving it, into the side of the bank with such force that it sounded like a bomb exploding. The next thing I know, people are running from the bank, thinking that the bank had been blown up.

Nutsey ran over to calm them down before someone called the cops. He told the bank manager that I was new on the job and that the explosion they heard was the container hitting the bank, nothing more. The manager looked at the truck for a moment and then he and the customers walked back into the bank. I unloaded the container on my second try.

Driving out of the parking lot, I think I was in the state of shock. The day just started, and I was a wreck. I was praying that the bad guys stop us, yank us out of the truck, and threaten us with bodily harm if we didn't stop driving for Dana. At least I'd be able to make an arrest and end the torture.

It took us all day to finish the route. We didn't get back to the yard until 6:30 P.M. Our eight-hour day had stretched into fifteen hours and Nutsey was mad as hell. Lucky for us, Nutsey had the key to the yard and we didn't have to call Jimmy to open the gate. He jumped out of the truck to open the gate, and said, "Frank, we don't get overtime! You gotta do better tomorrow!"

He unlocked the padlock and pushed each side of the chain link gate back, as I drove into the yard. I parked the truck in front of the garage and headed for my car. I turned back towards Nutsey and shouted, "I'll see ya in the morning."

He yelled back, "Okay, see ya in the morning." He got into his beat up Mustang, and slowly drove out. He waited for me to pull out. I saw Nutsey in the distance locking the gate as I drove up the street.

It was almost seven and I was hungry. I decided to stop at Sinapi's pizzeria just up the street from the yard. My phone rang. I glanced at the number. It was my Cousin Tommy's wife, Anna. She was crying hysterically. She told me Tommy had been shot. I could hear their two young kids crying in the background. "Anna, what happened?"

"Tommy was shot as he closed the gym last night. He's in intensive care at Montefiore Medical Center in the Bronx."

"Who shot him?"

"Alex Shivone. They call him Crazy Alex, an ex-boxer. Tommy told the Bronx cops that Shivone was shaking him down for free membership. But, you know Tommy; he stood up to him, and got himself shot."

"Anna, is he gonna be alright?"

"He lost a lot of blood, but the doctor said that he will be okay."

I breathed a sigh of relief. "That's good. Try to calm down. I'll keep on top of it, and tell my cousin not to worry, I'm gonna find the guy who shot him."

As soon as I got off the phone with Anna, Joe called. "Hey Frankie, how was your first day?"

"Fucking miserable."

"I'll make it short then. Howell assigned me to pick up your reports."

"Joey, that's great. But something personal just came up. Can we meet at Jakes later?"

"I'm at Jakes now."

"I'll be there in ten minutes."

I drove around the block a few times, looking in the rear view mirror to make sure that I wasn't being followed. At Jakes, Jessica was tending bar. I briefly stopped at the bar to say hi, ordered a burger medium rare, and a Guinness. Joe was in a booth, nursing a beer. I slid in, sitting across from him. He looked up and smiled. "Hey buddy. What's going on?"

Apparently Joe had already eaten. I leaned forward so no one could hear me and said, "Joey, I think I'm gonna need your help."

The waiter arrived, sliding beers in front of us. Smiling he said, "I'll be back with your burger." The anguish on my face was apparent. "So Frankie, tell me what's going on?"

"My Cousin Tommy was shot last night as he locked up his gym on White Plains Road in the Bronx. Some half-assed wise-guy was shaking him down for free membership. You know my cousin. He's like you, a hard headed Irishman that doesn't take shit from anybody. He stood up to this prick and got himself shot. I just got off the phone with Tommy's wife and told her that I'd help find the guy."

Joe took a gulp of his beer. "Frankie, whatever it takes, we'll find him." He lifted his glass, guzzled down the rest of the beer, wiped his lips, and said, "Is he gonna be okay?"

"I think so. He was shot in the stomach with a small caliber bullet. He's lost a lot of blood, but they think he'll pull through."

"Who shot him?"

"They call him Crazy Alex. He's an ex-boxer. His name is Alex Shivone. I gotta find out who this guy is."

The waiter walked over with my burger. Joe asked him to bring us two more beers. I dug into the burger and fries, and knocked back the Guinness. Jessica walked over from behind the bar. She sensed that something was wrong. Joe looked up and said, "Frankie's cousin Tommy was shot last night."

Jessica asked, "Is he going to be alright?"

I nodded yes.

Joe waived to the waiter for another round, but I motioned back, shaking my forefinger no, that I'd had enough. I told Joe that I had to get up in a few hours and didn't need a hangover. He said that he understood. Howell had briefed him on what I was doing. He chuckled and asked, "So you had a rough day, huh? And by the way, you stink."

Joe asked, "Should I tell Shake-N-Bake we met?"

"Yeah, tell him so far that the only thing I haven't hit with the truck is a human being." We both started laughing. It was late and I knew that I had to get home. "Joe, I'll keep you in the loop. I gotta do some research on this guy. When I get a line on Alex, I'll give you a call." I waved for the check, but Joe said he got it. Before leaving, I asked Joe if he'd run the criminal history on James Newcomb, a/k/a Shorty.

He replied, "Sure."

I also asked him to run a criminal check on Louis Fuganza, a/k/a Nutsey.

I later found out that Alex Shivone had a rap sheet a mile long. He's been locked up for assault, robbery, extortion, and last week, he battered his girlfriend so badly that it took six hours to put her arm back together. Alex is a connected guy. He's an enforcer for a known shy-lock, Little Artie Pisano, a soldier in the Colombo family.

As soon as I could, I called the detectives in the 47th precinct and asked if they were having any luck finding Alex. I got the impression that they weren't looking very hard. From what I understood, Alex dropped the gun at the scene. The gun was put into evidence, but now they can't find it. Through word on the street, Alex knows that Tom survived, and he's on the run. We're shaking the trees for information on his whereabouts, but so far, we're not coming up with anything. Our ace in the hole is that Joe has an informant who's close to Pisano. If we're lucky, we'll find out where Alex is hiding.

CHAPTER EIGHT

The piece of shit car that Howell assigned me almost didn't start. I was running late and didn't want to deal with Newcomb's ranting and raving. Luck was with me. I pulled into the yard fifteen minutes early. Nutsey was talking with a few of the other drivers. I figured that it might be a good idea to test the waters and ask one or two of the drivers to stop for a beer after work. I'd have them in a place where I could pump them about the murders. Dave was one of the drivers I met yesterday. He's a strapping guy in his mid-forties. I parked in the usual place and walked over to him as he was about to climb into his truck. I yelled to Dave to hold on, and casually asked him if he wanted to stop for a few beers after work.

"Sounds good Miranda. What do ya got in mind?"

I wanted him to let him pick the place. I replied, "I don't know. You tell me."

"Uh, there's a place on Yonkers Avenue called The Hole in the Wall. We stop there from time to time."

"Sounds good. Why don't you ask some of the other guys if they want to stop too?"

He chuckled and grinned. "Yeah, hopefully you'll be there before dark. If you don't show up, we'll know why."

Nutsey was waving me over, so I cut the conversation short. As I climbed into the cab and drove out of the yard, Nutsey was looking over the galley. On the ride to Rye, I told him that Dave was going to ask a few of the guys if they wanted to stop for a drink after work.

He lit a cigarette and stared at me for a moment. "Where ya goin?"

I replied, "We're goin to The Hole in the Wall. Nutsey was filling up the cab with cigarette smoke. I tapped his leg and said, "Nutsey, please roll down the window if you're gonna smoke. It's making me sick." He glared at me for a second, took a long drag on the cigarette, and rolled down the window.

"C'mon Nutsey, I got asthma, give me a break. By the way, do you want to join us for a beer?"

As he puffed way, he nodded yes and said, "Ah, sounds good, but it's up to you. If today's anything like yesterday, forget about it."

"Yeah, you're right."

I wanted to find out what made Nutsey tick. I asked, "So, Nutsey, where do ya live?"

"I live in Yonkers, the Parkhill section. How about you?"

"I live in the Bronx, Fordham."

"Yeah, how long?"

"A few years."

"Do you like living there?"

"Yeah, good Italian restaurants nearby."

Nutsey sat up as I was pulling off I-95. He looked relaxed and said, "So, you were in the landscaping business. What happened?"

"I lost it to a bigger company that undercut my prices."

"Yeah," he said, "I know these big companies. They'll eat you up alive. I've been picking up garbage for years, and see it all the time. The small independent companies don't have a chance."

"Yeah, especially when wise guys are concerned." He looked over at me as if afraid to say anything. I figured that I'd keep hammering him with questions. "So Nutsey, do you have a ten-year plan? Do you want to do something else? Get married? Have kids?"

He laughed, "Ten-year plan? Get married? Why would I want to do that?" He turned his head, looking out the window. "No, I'm not crazy. I don't want those problems. I want to stay where I am. I get good benefits, and I know my job. I just hope I don't get pushed off the truck."

I continued to press him. "Pushed off the truck, by who?"

Again he didn't answer. He just stared out the passenger window. As we continued down Theodore Fremd Avenue, Nutsey picked up the galley and said, "Our first stop is a dog kennel on North Street. We got a 150 yarder."

We got there in no time. I pulled up in front of Ballard's dog kennel. Nutsey stepped out of the truck to guide me back to the dumpster that was at the far end of the driveway. I began to feel nauseous. I wasn't used to the smell of diesel fuel. I managed to angle the truck, backing it up into the driveway. As I'm backing up, he's yelling, "C'mon back, c'mon back. Remember, the side view mirrors."

It must have been a miracle because I connected on my first try. Nutsey was smiling from ear to ear. I jumped out of the truck, and hooked the cable to the container. As I pulled the lever engaging the cable, the container started to rise slowly. Nutsey grabbed the handle that operates the hopper and pulled it, moving tons of dog shit into the truck. Then he said, "Frank, remember that we didn't dump at the transfer station yesterday, so the truck is full."

As the container lifted higher and higher, the dog shit slid into the hopper. All of a sudden I heard a loud snap. The cable wire snapped in two, sending the container crashing down to the ground with a loud bang. There was dog shit everywhere. I looked at Nutsey as if I'd been shot. I was hardly able to speak. I yelled, "Nutsey, I don't know what to do. I just don't know what to do. We're fucked!"

Nutsey dropped his head, shaking it in disgust. He looked around at the mess in disbelief and finally said, "Yeah, we're fucked alright."

He ran to the side of the truck, grabbing two shovels from one of the compartments on the underside of the truck. "I know what we're going to do," he snapped. We're gonna pick up the dog shit! Grab a fucking shovel!" We began shoveling the dog shit into the truck. Then Nutsey said glumly, "We gotta call Shorty." I put my shovel down and shot a call to Shorty. Naturally, he wasn't happy. He told me that he'd send someone out to replace the cable.

We didn't talk much as we shoveled the shit into the hopper. The smell was overwhelming. The mechanic finally arrived three hours later, replacing the cable in less than thirty minutes. We headed for the transfer station on Oakland Beach Avenue, dumping our prized load.

The galley showed that our next pick up was Carpet Trends, a retail carpet store on Smith Street. It's off Purchase Street where all the shops and stores are located. As we continued on Purchase Street, he pointed to Carpet Trends, which fronts on Smith Street. "Cheech, pull behind the store, the dumpster's there."

I drove into the parking lot at the back of the store. Some guy who looked like he had steam shooting out from his ears, came running out of the rear of the store, mad as hell, told us that we need to pick up the scraps of carpet left on the ground from our last pick up. The guy's ranting on that they pay for a clean pick up and they shouldn't have to clean up after us. He didn't stop, and got into Nutsey's face. I had enough of his bullshit. I got out of the truck, grabbed him by the shoulder, and spun him around. "Fuck you, you fucking fuck. Who do you think you are?"

Nutsey lunged between us, pushing us apart. This guy was stunned. He took a few steps back, and decided that it was in his best interest to calm down. "I'm the store manager, Allen Rogers. The owner wants it clean. That's how he runs things."

I stepped back and took a deep breath. "If you got any complaints, call the office." I then settled myself, and got back into the truck. Nutsey went about picking up the scraps of carpet, and throwing them into the hopper.

Garbage Murders

It was my second day on the job, and besides a few snafus, I was really getting the hang of it. I gotta tell you, it felt good. I started to feel like a garbage man.

We arrived back at the yard at about five. I noticed an unmarked police car parked behind one of the garbage trucks. After filling the truck with diesel fuel, I pulled it into the garage. Nutsey walked to his car and I gave him a wink. I'm really getting to like this guy. I was about to get into my car, when I saw Newcomb rush out of the office and get into a late model, two-door, baby blue Cadillac Eldorado. There was definitely something going on in the office. My curiosity got the best of me and I wanted to know what it was. I took the 9 millimeter from my waist, tucked it under the front seat of my car, and headed up the stairs to the office. I heard a clamoring of voices. A male voice resounded above the rest. "You know a lot more than you're telling us!"

A woman cried out. "No, I don't. Please believe me."

I knocked on the door and walked in. Dana was seated on the couch. A large male was shouting at her. "That's bull shit, that's bull shit!" Another male stood off to the side, his arms crossed, looking like he wanted to bite someone's head off. They didn't expect me to walk in.

I reacted and cried out, "What the fuck is going on?"

I found out later, they were New Rochelle Detectives Straub and Barry. Straub reared back, rushing me. He spun me around and cranked my arm at a right angle towards my shoulder. Detective Barry followed in suit. They threw me up against the wall. The weight of both bodies on mine, immobilized me. Detective Straub drew his hand gun and stuck the barrel up against my temple shouting, "Get up against the wall! Get up against the wall!"

His hand was shaking. From the corner of my eye, I could see his finger was resting on the trigger. I hollered, "I am against the wall. Do you want me to go up or down? I'll do whatever you say but please take the gun off my head."

Dana was in shock. She sat there motionless. Detective Barry sensing that things could get ugly, took hold of Straub's forearm, forcing him to lower the pistol. Detective Straub was screaming in my ear. "Who the fuck are you?" He then dragged me over to the desk, pushing my face down.

Dana begged. "Please don't hurt him. He didn't do anything."

I felt the edge of nausea rush through me. "I'm Frank Miranda, I work here. Who are you guys?"

Detective Barry patted me down, looking for weapons. Straub released his hold, as he and Detective Barry identified themselves. They shouted, "New Rochelle PD." Straub took my wallet out of my pocket and tossed it on the desk. He removed my driver's license and examined it. He wrote my personal information down on a 3x5 note pad and mumbled, "Um, Hughes Avenue, Bronx."

"Yes. I live on Hughes Avenue."

Detective Straub then threw my license in my face. It fell to the floor as he said, "Next time, mind your business." As they were leaving, Detective Barry looked back, and took a parting shot. "Dana, this is not over. We'll be back."

Dana stood. Then she sat back down sobbing. I walked over. She looked up, gesturing with her hand for me to sit. Her voice cracking as she continued sobbing. "Frank, I'm sorry. Are you okay?"

My eyes focused on hers, I replied, "Yeah, I'm fine. Those guys are fucking nuts."

She slid her hand on my leg, and pushed up against me. "Since Gary's murder, I've been alone....... I need...."

I stopped her, placing my forefinger up to her lips. "Dana, you're a beautiful woman, but I'm committed to someone, and I don't want to ruin it."

Her hand slid off of me, as if trying to understand what I just said. She moved away. "She's lucky to have you."

I took her hand and gently pulled her up from the couch. "Look, Dana, I'm here for you. We'll work through this thing together."

I left her standing there and walked out of the office, not quite believing what just happened. It was late, and I wanted to go straight home. But, the thought crossed my mind that the New Rochelle cops might be waiting in the street to follow me. I had to be careful. It's hard to pick up a tail at night, and I didn't want to be followed to my apartment in Bronxville. I unlocked the car and looked around the yard and then got in. I slowly pulled out onto Fourth Street. The only thing out of the ordinary was Dana's white Mercedes, parked across the street.

As I drove out of the yard, I saw a set of headlights turn on and pull out behind me. The car was about a half block away. Making a right turn onto Lockwood Avenue, I looked into my rear view mirror to see if the car was still behind me. It was. I thought, if the car makes the left with me onto Webster Avenue, I was in for the ride of my life. Sure enough the car made the left. I couldn't make the car out. The only thing I could see was its headlights. I began to speed up on Webster Avenue, heading for the Cross County Parkway. The car behind me also accelerated and was now only a few hundred feet behind. I got onto the parkway southbound, heading for the Bronx. By the time I hit the Bronx line, we must have been driving at ninety miles an hour, weaving in and out of traffic.

I wasn't sure if it was the New Rochelle cops or maybe it's the people who want Dana's business. No matter who it is, they're going to get the surprise of their life if they can stop me. I reached for my 9 millimeter under the front seat, sliding it along side of me. I looked in the rear view mirror to see who was chasing me, but was unable to make out who it was. In any event, I mean to put the fear of God into them, if I can find out who it is.

I headed for the Westchester Avenue exit, hoping I'd lose them in the Bronx. My adrenalin was pumping. My heart raced, as thoughts of a confrontation tumbled through my mind. I was holding the steering wheel so tightly that my hands were numb. I'd be lucky if it didn't snap in two.

The Cadillac was holding up just fine, and its big eight-cylinder engine was giving the prick behind me a run for his money. I could see that the exit for Westchester Avenue was coming fast. I was now passing other cars like they were standing still. I knew when I took the exit, I'd have to slow down and make a quick left onto the access road leading out to Westchester Avenue.

I took the exit at about sixty miles per hour, spinning around the turn on two wheels, and nearly sideswiping several parked cars. The shithead behind me wasn't so lucky. As he attempted the turn onto Westchester Avenue, he crashed into one of the massive steel girders that supports the elevated trains. The impact could be heard several blocks away. I stopped for a moment and looked back at the car as it smoldered.

The smartest thing for me to do was to keep going. I just wanted to go home and wash the stink of dog shit off me. The adrenalin rush almost blinded me. I could hardly see the road ahead. Fortunately, I saw the entrance of the parkway. My phone rang as soon as I got onto the parkway, it was Denise. I took a short breath, and in a shaky voice said. "I'm fine hon. I'm on my way home."

She sounded relieved to hear my voice and sighed, "Good. I'm a little tired. Do you want me to wait up for you?"

At this point the only thing that I could think of was wrapping my hands around a glass of Cognac. I replied, "Only if you want to. I need a drink."

From the sound of my voice she sensed that something was wrong. "Darling, are you sure you're okay?"

"I'm fine. Not to worry."

"Okay, please hurry home." The word home has such meaning for me. It's more than an apartment where I live, eat and sleep. It's where the heart is. My divorce from Helen was brutal. It forced me to leave my home and kids. There's not a night that goes by that I don't think of them. Now, I'm living with Denise and finally found a place where everything seems to fit. It's a place where I don't have to pretend to be someone else.

Tomorrow will come soon enough, but tonight, I can go home, and for a little while escape the pressures of the job.

CHAPTER NINE

Sure enough, the alarm sounded at 2:00 A.M. Denise rolled over and asked if I was awake. I sat on the end of the bed, holding my head in my hands. I muttered, "I'm awake, I'll try to be quiet."

Denise turned back on her stomach mumbling, "Be careful, I love you."

I pulled myself up, grabbed my clothes, and dressed. Before leaving, I took an extra clip for my nine millimeter, checked to see that my pistol was loaded, and slipped it into my waist. Quietly, I closed the bedroom door and walked into the living room. I noticed that I'd left the bottle of Cognac sitting on the coffee table, and thought that it might not be a bad idea to take it with me. Maybe a nip or two just might take the edge off driving that monstrosity of a garbage truck.

As I said, I love the quiet in the early morning hours. The peace it brings me gives me the energy to ease into the day. Believe it or not, the ride over to the yard is therapeutic. When I pulled into the yard, Jimmy was talking with one of the drivers. As I locked my car, he waved me over. I could feel his treacherous eyes studying me as I walked over. "Frank, I heard what those fucking cops did last night. Dana called me. They think they got a license to push people around."

Looming over him I looked squarely in his eyes. "Yeah, Shorty, they got a license alright. I say, screw them where they breathe."

Newcomb got up close to me, looking like he wanted to convey a message. "Nobody talks to the cops. Got it? And I told you don't call me Shorty!"

At that moment, a flash of light went off in my head. I wondered if it was Newcomb, or someone he had sent to follow me last night.

Newcomb wasn't giving anything away by the way he spoke. I smiled and looked at him like he had two heads. I shot back at this unemotional nasty little prick, "Sure Shorty, nobody talks to the cops." Right then, my only wish was that someday I'd be able to put the cuffs on the little cretin. He squinted like he had splinters in his eyes. The weasel screamed at the top of his lungs, "I thought I told you never to call me Shorty! What are you, the village idiot? What don't you understand? Only my close friends call me Shorty, and as I've said many times, you're not my friend!"

I looked at Nutsey who was sheepishly standing by the truck, then at Newcomb. I replied sarcastically, "Look, Nutsey is waiting for me. We'll straighten this out another time," and walked away. Brushing past Dave, I huffed, "See you at The Hole in the Wall about three thirty."

He shook his head yes and with a slight grin replied, "Hope you can make it tonight."

Nutsey was in the truck as I climbed in. He was looking over the galley. Before starting the engine, I jumped out of the truck and ran to my car, grabbing the bottle of Cognac from the front seat. I hustled back into the truck taking a large swig. I handed the bottle to Nutsey, but he refused it, shaking his head no. "It's too early to drink."

I threw back another hefty swallow, turned on the ignition, and drove out of the yard. Nutsey was fumbling with the galley, mumbling, "Our first stop is Kmart in Port Chester. They've got a 150 yarder of cardboard and paper."

I looked over and nodded. I was still fuming from my run in with Newcomb. I wanted to get off this truck in the worst way. It seemed to me that my only way off was to solve the murders. I braced Nutsey straight up. "Nutsey, why is it that nobody talks about Gary and Lenny's murders? It's like business as usual."

Nutsey looked like I kicked him in the balls. He then said, "Shorty told everybody not to talk about it, and he meant it. As you can see, he's the type of guy that'll cut your balls off and make you eat them."

I laughed to get his attention. "Well answer me this, who would want them dead?"

I could barely hear him. He was talking low like there was someone else in the truck. "The other garbage companies would make out like a bandit. That's all I know. I don't want to talk about it. Why do you keep asking me?"

"I don't know. As I said, I'm just curious."

I noticed that Nutsey was twitching. As I drove off I-95 into Port Chester, Kmart was in the shopping center right off the exit. Nutsey excitedly took off his skullcap, motioning to the store with his hat. He told me to drive to the back of the store. I could see that his twitch was getting worse. His head shook like one of those bobble head dolls. Nutsey was about to get out of the truck. I asked him, "Are you okay? You're shaking like a leaf."

A cigarette hung from his mouth as his body shook. He looked over at me and laughed, "Yeah, I'm okay. I forgot to take my medicine." He jumped out of the truck shouting, "Cheech, remember to use the side view mirrors."

I slowly backed the truck towards the container and felt the truck gently come to rest against it. I yelled from the cab, "Nutsey am I in?"

He shook his head no as if to say here we go again. "No. No you're not. Try it again."

I couldn't help myself. I reached for the bottle of Cognac, and took two big gulps. It burned a little on the way down, but it tasted good. I'm not sure, but I think it gave me the edge I needed to drive this fucking thing. I pulled up, straightened the truck out, and started back. Nutsey was flipping around like he had Saint Vitus Dance. I stopped the truck and asked him, "How about a hit of Cognac? Maybe it will calm you down!"

He shrugged his shoulders, "Yeah, maybe." He walked over, grabbed the bottle and swallowed almost a quarter of it. Wiping his mouth with the sleeve of his shirt, he grinned and said, "Thanks, I needed that."

As I inched back, I could feel the truck bump up against the container, but this time connecting. Nutsey yelled, "You're in! Cheech, you're in!" I jumped out of the truck and hooked up the cable as fast as I could, then slowly raised the container. The loose cardboard slipped into the hopper like a greased pig as Nutsey maintained the flow of cardboard into the truck. I then slowly lowered it to the ground. Nutsey pulled himself up into the cab with a shit-eating grin. "That's the way to do it. I think you've got it down now."

The next ten stops went without a hitch. And I didn't need another hit of Cognac for support. It was eleven o'clock and we headed for the Town & Country Coffee Shop. I turned onto Midland Avenue and immediately saw the coffee shop up the street. No sooner had I made the turn, when Nulligan called. "Cheech, can you meet me at Jake's tonight? It's important. Howell and Friedman want me to brief you on what's going on with the homicide investigations."

"Sure, what time?"

"How about 8:30 P.M?"

Nutsey got out of the truck and asked if I wanted anything. "I'll have a coffee and a bagel." I reached into my wallet to give him five bucks, but he shook his head no.

I asked Joe, "By the way, any news on Shivone?"

"Yeah, I was saving it until tonight. But since you asked, my informant has been pumping Pisano for information. We should know something in a few days."

"That's good. Tommy and his wife are scared to death. We'll talk tonight."

I was getting used to the smell of the diesel fumes. Nutsey wasn't gone long. He rushed back into the cab holding a brown paper bag. He dug into the bag, pulled out a Danish and coffee for himself, and a buttered bagel and coffee for me. I couldn't help looking at Nutsey. Every time he took a bite of the Danish he grunted, and he has a habit of wiping his mouth with his shirt sleeve. The guy reminded me of a barnyard animal at feeding time. I couldn't help it and had to say something. "Ah, well, Nutsey, by the way you sucked down the Danish and coffee, it's like you haven't eaten in weeks."

He laughed and continued to drink his coffee, slurping as he drank it. Nutsey was anxious and wanted to get going. "C'mon Frank, we need to go and get rid of this shit. I want to finish by three today."

"Okay Nutsey." I downed my coffee, finished the bagel and headed to the transfer station.

The transfer station was a stones throw away on Oakland Beach Avenue. It took us a few minutes to dump the load. Our next pick up was a fifty yarder at the Hess station on Theodore Fremd. We were a few miles from the station. The Hess sign was visible from a block away. Nutsey took one last drag from his cigarette as I pulled into the gas station. He said, "The container is on the left side of the building, go slow, and take it easy around the pumps."

I stopped the truck to get the lay of the land. It was a tight squeeze between the pumps and the front of the station's building. Once I was satisfied that I knew how I was going to tackle the container, I put the truck in first gear and slowly headed towards the container. I made sure that I was using the side view mirrors to avoid hitting anything, especially the pumps. As I inched my way around the gas pumps, I heard a horrific crunching sound like metal bending. I immediately slammed the air brakes down, almost sending them through the floor. I began to hyperventilate as I frantically looked around the station for anything that I might have hit. "Nutsey, I don't see anything."

Nutsey had a twenty mission stare.

At this point, my hands were rapped so tightly around the steering wheel, my knuckles were turning white. It would take a crowbar to pry my hands loose. "Did you hear that? Did you hear that crunch?"

Nutsey was overwhelmed with fear, clumsily reaching into the air as he scanned the station for anything I might have hit.

I pulled the truck forward slowly. The crunching sound got louder. "Nutsey, for Christ's sake, did you hear that?"

"Yeah. I heard it." Nutsey was frantically bouncing around the cab. He yelled, "For God sakes, be careful."

My foot pressed hard on the brakes, I was becoming unhinged. I barked, "Nutsey, I looked left! I looked fucking right! There's nothing there!"

Nutsey was flailing like he had fleas. His eye lids were blinking so fast I thought he was going to pass out. He shouted, "I don't see anything. Cheech, you're okay. You're okay. Go slow!"

I put the truck in gear again and slowly inched it forward. As soon as the truck moved we both heard the same sound of metal bending and tearing, e-e- e- e- e-, then a loud explosion, and a flash of bright light like we were in the middle of an atomic bomb exploding. I felt the ground shake. We looked at each other with our mouths hung open, unable to speak. We were both in the state of shock. I looked over at Nutsey. The thought running through my mind was that we were going to be burned alive. Within in a millisecond, the office door flew open; a guy comes running out screaming at the top of his lungs, "What did you do? Oh my God! Oh my God! What did you do?"

The sudden realization, that I tore off the overhead fluorescents lights above the pumps with the top front end of the truck, shook me to my core. The guy looked around at the debris from the overhead light lying all over the ground, and held his head in his hands, howling like a wounded dog.

When I was finally able to say something, I choked out the words, "Nutsey, I looked left, I looked right. Nobody told me to fucking look up!"

Thank God for small favors. The pumps didn't catch fire. By now Nutsey was emotionally deflated. He slowly got out of the truck and walked over to the guy on the ground, and tried to console him. He yelled, "Cheech, you gotta call Shorty! You gotta call Newcomb! He's gonna kill us!"

Nutsey lifted the guy up, and helped him into the office. I later found out that he owned the gas station. It was time to face the music. I climbed out of the truck and walked into the office. I tried to calm the guy down by telling him not to worry. The company's insurance would cover of everything, but he didn't seem to hear me. He just walked around the office muttering, "I can't believe it, I just can't believe it."

Nutsey stood there hunched over, silent, leaning against the wall. I knew I had to call Newcomb, and give him the bad news. I asked if I could use the phone. The station owner, plopped himself down at his desk, and rolled his head towards the phone on the desk. "Make the call."

I took one long deep breath before I dialed Newcomb's number. I began to tell him what happened, but he couldn't spit the words out fast enough, and cut me off. "You what? The fluorescent lights? I'm gonna cut your fucking balls off Miranda! Miranda, that's it! No more! Get back to the yard!"

I looked over at Nutsey, who had a blank stare on his face. "But Jimmy, I got four or five more stops."

He cut me off again. "I'm sending another truck to finish!" and he slammed down the phone.

Nutsey and I walked out of the office, miserable. I can't speak for Nutsey, but I was mentally beaten. Climbing back into the truck, I grabbed the bottle of Cognac and knocked down what was left in the bottle. From the look on Nutsey's face, I knew I was in deep shit.

Jimmy was in the office when I drove into the yard. He came running out as soon we got out of the truck. He ran up to me, "You stupid son-of-a-bitch." Without another word he jumped up, straddling me with his legs, and began choking me. I could see the hatred spewing out of the cocksucker's eyes. A few of the guys ran over to try to separate us. But Jimmy wouldn't have it. He continued to choke me. "You're an idiot! You're a fucking idiot! The damages are coming out of your pay!"

I was trying to shake him off me, but he was wrapped so tightly around me I couldn't. He was so in my face, I could smell the garlic he had for lunch. Then the little motherfucker slid his head down and bit me in the neck. At that point, I was able to slide one arm under his, angling it up, forcing his head back, and grabbing his throat. I was able to slide my other arm between my chest and his belly, forcing my arm down to his nuts, and grabbing hold of them. I squeezed them so hard that I swear I heard them pop. He yelped like a mad dog, releasing his hold, I threw him to the ground as hard as I could. I stood over him, about to kick the prick into the street, but somehow I was able to regain my composure. My neck was throbbing. I reached up to see if he had drawn blood. Thank God there wasn't any. This back stabbing excuse for a human being was rolling around in the dirt yelping like a wounded animal. "You bit me you little fuck. You're lucky I don't kill you now."

All I could think about was getting away from him, and putting some antiseptic on my neck. I walked away leaving him on the ground, in a fetal position, holding his balls, and moaning. I had to think of a way to get even with this scumbag. But for now, I had to find a drug store and buy some hydrogen peroxide. I needed to find a liquor store to buy another bottle of Cognac to self medicate.

I found the first aid I needed in a strip mall a few blocks away on North Avenue. After dousing my neck with peroxide, I decided to head over to The Hole in the Wall for a drink. I certainly could use one, and it didn't make a difference if any of the drivers showed up.

As soon as I left the strip mall and pulled into traffic Dana called. "Hey Frank, I heard what happened. Are you alright?"

I was surprised that she found out so quickly. "Who called you?"
I could hear the concern in her voice. "It doesn't matter who called. I just want to make sure that you're okay."

"I'm fine, but Newcomb's insane. What's wrong with the guy?"

"Frankly, you've cost me a lot of money with all the damage you're doing. My insurance premium is going up. But Newcomb is only looking out for me. I'll admit it, he gets carried away sometimes, but please don't quit. I'll talk to him."

"I ain't goin anywhere."

I had to laugh. She was right. I must be costing her a fortune. Dana and I talked for several more minutes, and I reassured her of my resolve to stay with the investigation to the end. Dana said that she didn't know how to thank me for sticking my neck out, and she would make it up to me in some way. I told her that I was just doing my job and that she had nothing to make up for.

CHAPTER TEN

The Hole in the Wall is a dingy little bar located in a commercial/ residential area in North Yonkers. The joint is so small that I had to squeeze by a pool table to get to the bar. Dave was standing at the bar drinking a beer. He nodded as I walked over and said, "Hey, I heard you had a run-in with Shorty."

"Word travels fast. Who told you?"

"One of the guys called me. He told me that you left Shorty rolling around on the ground moaning and holding his nuts. "

I gave Dave a friendly slap on the back. "The guy will never put his hands on me again."

Looking into his drink, he shook his head and said, "I get it."

I noticed that the bartender was sniffing the air as I pulled up a stool. I guess he could smell the scent of garbage on our clothes, something I was getting used to and didn't notice. The bartender needed a shave, and good dentist to clean the plaque buildup on his teeth.

Looking around the place, I could see why it's called the The Hole in the Wall. Six small tables and chairs covered in red plastic take up the entire room, with the exception of the pool table. It doesn't look like the oak floors have been swept in months. There's dirt everywhere.

Dave asked me what I was drinking. "I'll have a Guinness, if they have it."

The bartender finally lifted his head making some sort of animal sound. "We got Guinness in the bottle, okay?"

I nodded yes. "Sure that's fine."

The bartender looked like he was doing me a favor by reaching under the bar to grab the bottle of beer, and asking if I wanted a glass. *A glass? I wouldn't drink out of a glass here even if he held a pistol to my head.* God only knows what virus could be growing on it. The only thing he seemed interested in was watching the Yankee's vs. Boston on the flat screen TV that hung over the bar. He forced himself to look at me and ask, "Do you want to run a tab? It's $2.75 a bottle."

"Yeah, run a tab. No glass, and give my friend Dave another beer."

This was the first time I saw Dave not wearing his ski cap. His hair was a mess and needed cutting. Dave seemed like the kind of guy who didn't talk much, so I decided to break the ice. "I can't believe Newcomb. I had an accident. What's up with him?"

Dave looked over grinning. "Nobody's done the damage you've done."

I just shrugged my shoulders, with a look of so what, and chugged half the bottle of beer down. Nutsey walked in and pulled up a stool. I shook his hand as he sat down. "Nutsey, what are you drinking? I'm running a tab."

The bartender glanced over at Nutsey and said, "Hey, Nutsey, the usual?"

Nutsey rolled his shirt sleeves up. "Yeah George, pour me a mug of Bass Ale."

George forced his fat ass off the stool and poured a glass of the ale from the tap. He then slid it over to Nutsey. "Here you go Nutsey."
Nutsey cocked his head, shooting him a smile. "Thanks, George."

Dave quickly finished the rest of his Miller Light and slid the empty glass over to George. "Fill it up."

"Hey George, while you're up, back everyone up with another beer." I said with a smile. He looked like I asked him to run the New York City Marathon.

Nutsey, who seldom takes his skullcap off, threw it in on the bar. "Frank, you gotta be careful of Shorty. After what happened today, he'll try to hurt you."

Dave nudged me and said, "There's reasons why you've got to be careful now. For one, you've made a fool out of him in front of some of the guys. And two, don't let his size fool you. He's mean and treacherous. I've heard he's stuck a few guys with an ice pick in bar fights. You'd better watch your back."

I'm thinking, as I rubbed the area on my neck where he bit me, *I'll watch my back alright, and Shorty had better watch his.* I got the feeling that Nutsey and Dave liked me. After a few beers we were feeling comfortable, so I figured I'd ask them about Gary and Lenny's murder. "So, why do you think that Gary and his partner were killed?"

They both looked at each other like they wanted to back away from my question. There was something about their reluctance to talk about it that bothered me. Maybe they were afraid that Shorty would find out that they were talking to me about the murders. Dave turned to me, putting his forefinger to his lips as if to say be quiet. "Some things you don't want to talk about. Besides, what's it to you anyway?"

I looked at him, shrugging my shoulders and said smugly, "Uh, well, it was in the newspapers. And besides, we're in the middle things. Drivers are being forced to quit, and it's obvious that someone wants Dana's business."

Nutsey inadvertently said what he was thinking. "I heard Gary's father, Carmine, telling Dana that he's going to kill the people responsible for his son's death, and that she should sell the business back to him. It's too much for her to handle."

Now that Nutsey opened the door and spoke about Gary's murder, Dave began to talk too. "Gary and his father argued a lot, but after all, we all know who Carmine is, and Gary was his flesh and blood. I wouldn't want to be in the shoes of the people who did this."

"Dave, what'd they disagree about?" I asked. Dave replied, "Carmine didn't like how Gary and Lenny were running the business. Carmine didn't think that they were charging enough for the stops."

Nutsey then blurted out, "One day, I heard Gary and his father yelling at each other. Gary didn't like the way his father treated his mother."

I pressed them for more information. "Why do you think that Dana doesn't want to sell the business back to Carmine?"

Nutsey, who was now well oiled with alcohol replied, "She feels that Gary and Lenny built the business up after three years of hard work and it's finally making money. It's their legacy. She feels if she keeps the business going, somehow Gary won't be forgotten."

I nodded my head as if I understood. I thought I'd gotten as much information from them as I could. I called out to George for the check. Nutsey and Dave started to reach into their pockets, but I stopped them. "Guys, I'm the new boy on the block. It's my treat." I took out forty dollars from my wallet, and handed it to George. I told him to keep the change. The pencil neck prick's eyes lit up as he stuffed the money in his pocket, instead of putting it in the cash register. I told the guys that I'd see them in the morning.

CHAPTER ELEVEN

It was 6:30 P.M. and I still had to meet Nulligan. I gave him a call and asked if we could meet me earlier than planned. Joe was still at the office doing paperwork on several Oxycodone buys he made from some quack doctor. The doctor was writing prescriptions for Oxycodone like he was handing out free tickets to a Yankee game. Joe said that he was just finishing up. He'd meet me at Jake's in thirty minutes.

On my way to the bar, my Cousin Tommy called. He sounded upset. He'd been out the hospital for a week, and was at home recuperating. "Tommy, what's wrong?"

"It's that fuck, Alex. He found out where I live and threw a brick through the windshield of my car. On the front seat he left a note for me not to testify."

I didn't say anything. I just listened.

"Anna is scared to death for me and the kids. She thinks he'll hurt the kids. We've moving upstate to her mother's house. Frankie, you gotta find him before he finds me."

"Tommy, get out of the Bronx as fast as you can. I'll find him."

Jake's was crowded when I walked in. The bar and dining room were full. I looked for an empty booth, and noticed that Jessica wasn't working. Bobby McCarthy was tending bar. Bobby has worked at Jake's for almost twenty years. He's a good looking guy, in his late forties, with riveting blue eyes, and has a great personality. He looks like he should be tending bar on Waikiki beach. His gift of gab has attracted a large following. Not taking anything away from Jessica, but Bobby brings in a lot of customers.

A waitress was cleaning off a table and waved me over. Before I had a chance to sit down, Bobby had a Guinness in front of me. The waitress asked if I was planning to eat. I took a gulp of the beer, wiped the beer suds off of my mustache, and nodded yes. I ordered two baskets of hot chicken wings. I figured that I'd share the wings with Joe. The wings are delicious. They're deep fried in vegetable oil. The chef throws a large dollop of butter in a frying pan and adds hot sauce. He then throws in the wings, sautéing them for two minutes, and serves them up.

Joe walked in and saw me sitting in one of the booths. He walked over, and slid in, sitting across from me. He immediately began to sniff the air, trying to find the stench. Looking over at me, he smiled, and began to laugh, "You smell like my garbage can."

I just looked at him and didn't say anything. He knew that I didn't appreciate his humor at the moment. I'm thinking, if he only knew what kind of day I had he wouldn't be making those comments. Joe saw that my glass was almost empty, and yelled to Bobby, "I'll have a Blue Point, and Frankie will have another Guinness."

"Joe we gotta get to Alex soon. He knows where Tommy lives, and has been terrorizing him."

"We should know something soon. My informant is trying to pin down where Alex is hold up."

He raised his glass, chugged down half of the beer, and wiped the beer foam from his chin. Then he dug into the wings. "Wow, they're spicy. Cheech, "I got the criminal histories on Newcomb and Fuganza. Other than a few scraps as a kid, Fuganza is clean, but Newcomb, he's another story. He has a sheet as long as your arm."

My eyes lit up. "You don't say? That little fuck just bit me on the neck a half hour ago."

"He what?"

"You heard me. He bit me on the neck."

Chuckling he said, "Huh Frank, you gotta tell me what happened?"

"I had a little accident with the truck today and the hair bag went nuts, jumped up on me, and bit me on the neck."

Joe tried to stop laughing, but he couldn't, and spit out a mouthful of beer. "You've got to be kidding me."

"No, I'm not kidding you. But I'll bet the little prick is still rubbing his balls."

"You kicked him in the balls?"

"No, I squeezed his nuts so hard that they popped."

Joe was rolling in the booth from laughter. Whoever coined that phrase, *laughter is like medicine*, was right. It took my mind off Alex for a while. After a minute or so, Joe was able to compose himself. He took a deep breath, "Sorry, but that was funny. So anyway, here's what I got on Newcomb."

Joe took out a piece of notebook paper from his shirt pocket and began reading. "James Newcomb, a/k/a Shorty, was born in 1969. That makes him 35. He was born in Bronx, Lebanon Hospital, to Maureen and Jack Newcomb. His father is deceased and his mother, age 65, resides at 108 Rumsey Road in Yonkers, second floor apartment. Newcomb now lives in the Bronx, at 654 White Plains Road, Apt. 6J. I checked with New York State Bureau of Vital Statistics and he's never been married. He lives with a woman named Jean Miller, age 32. She signed the lease for the apartment. The telephone is listed in her name."

Joe took a gulp of beer, leaning forward, his elbows resting on the booth as he continued to read. "Frankie, now for the good stuff. On December 18, 1984, Newcomb was arrested by the 47th precinct in the Bronx for petit larceny. He stole a bicycle from a private house on Boston Road. On May 6, 1988, numb-nuts was arrested again by the 47th precinct for grand theft auto. He did six months in Rikers Island. On March 21, 1991, he was arrested by the Yonkers Police Department for possession of an eighth of an ounce of marijuana. He pleaded no contest and was sentenced to six months' probation. Then on June 6, 1996, he was arrested in a multi- agency gambling investigation, conducted by the New York State Police, New York City Police Department and the Westchester County District Attorneys Office. He was charged with felony possession and felony promotion of gambling. He pleaded guilty and did a year in Sing-Sing State Prison. He's got nothing after that pinch, but at the time of his last arrest, our Intelligence Squad had him working for Joseph Merino, a soldier in the Genovese family. Frankie, the guy's a player."

"The son-of- a- bitch is rubbing elbows with bad guys."

Joe nodded yes. "Yeah, I even ran a credit check on him. The guy doesn't pay his bills."

Joe reared his head back, like he was trying to remember something. "Oh, Friedman and Howell are getting a lot of pressure from Hogan to get these homicides solved. The investigations are cold. Howell told me to make sure to tell you that he needs you come up with something soon, or he's gonna pull you off the truck."

I looked at Joe for a second, shaking my head. "What's he think, I'm Harry Houdini? He's sitting behind his desk, fat and happy, making demands on me, because he's getting pressure from Hogan." I leaned forward, so no one could hear me. "Uh, you can tell that empty suit that I got a score to settle with Barry and Straub. They're cowboys. And another thing, tell him, whoever ends up with Corso Carting is responsible for the murders. Proving it is another thing."

Joe seemed to be wrestling with what I just told him. "What do ya mean cowboys?"

"Straub stuck his pistol up against my fucking head."
Joe didn't say anything. He just looked at me as if to say, *you gotta be kidding me.*

It was time to go. I stood and stretched out my hand. "I gotta go. I have to get up in a few hours."

Joe shook my hand as he motioned to the waitress for the check. She rushed over smiling. "Bobby has taken care of the check." Before walking out, I told Joe to keep me posted on Alex and thanked Bobby for picking up the tab.

CHAPTER TWELVE

It was 2:30 A.M. Thousands of stars lit up the sky as I left my apartment. For some reason I was eager to jump into my car and drive into New Rochelle. Unfortunately for me, the quiet of the early morning hours would soon end. I drove down Fourth Street, flames and smoke billowed up into the night sky. As I got closer to the yard, I realized that the fire was coming from Corso Carting. I pulled to the curb, parked down the street from the yard and walked up to the front gate. The fire was coming from a burning garbage truck. A number of firemen were hosing down the burning truck with fire hose attached to a hydrant in the street. Smoke from burning tires choked the air, making it hard to breathe. I noticed that the padlock on the front gate was cut, probably by a bolt cutter. The video surveillance camera was disabled. It wasn't until 3:30 A.M. that the fire was brought under control.

Just as the firemen were wrapping things up, Newcomb's tires screeched, as his car came to a stop in front of the main gate. He jumped out of the Cadillac, leaving it double parked in the street behind two marked New Rochelle police cars, with their emergency lights flashing. It just amazed me how Newcomb had his Cadillac altered so that he could drive it. He had wooden blocks, somehow affixed to the brake and gas peddles. His front seat was jacked up with a foam cushion, so he could see over the steering wheel.

Newcomb ran past me into the yard, as he shot me a sour look. I followed him into the yard and overheard the fire captain tell Newcomb that the fire was suspicious and most likely arson. The police placed yellow tape around the smoldering garbage truck and told the drivers who'd arrived to stay away from the truck. It was a crime scene.

As soon as the firemen and the cops left, Newcomb got all the drivers together in the maintenance garage. He told us that we would be splitting up the stops of the downed truck, and handed each driver the addresses of six additional stops in Greenwich, Connecticut. He told everyone to be careful, in light of what had just taken place. He mentioned that it's obvious that someone is trying to shut Dana down. He told Nick, the driver of the torched truck, that he'd be paid until they can replace the damaged truck. In front of everyone, Newcomb pointed to me, and said, "If it were up to me, Miranda, I'd fire your ass, and we wouldn't have to rush to replace Nick's truck."

If the fuck was trying to embarrass me or get some reaction, it didn't work. I gave him a look that would put a shiver up any normal person's spine, laughed and said, "I love you too, Jimmy."

The drivers tried to hold their laughter in but they couldn't.

As Newcomb walked out of the garage, he mumbled, "Let's see what you can hit today Miranda."

We were all on high alert and obviously upset about the truck being torched. I rubbed the butt of my 9 millimeter tucked in my waist under my sweatshirt. Knowing it was there, made me feel a lot better. As we climbed into the truck, I could see that Nutsey was upset. He muttered, "It's not going to stop until they shut her down."

I started the truck and looked over. "It looks that way."

I slowly pulled out of the yard and glanced at what was left of Nick's truck. It was still smoldering. Someone is sending Dana a direct message. They want her out of the carting business. Truthfully, things were escalating fast, and she should think about selling it before she gets hurt.

Nutsey lit a cigarette, rolling his eyes as I took a hit of Cognac. He pulled the sheet of paper with the extra stops out of his sweatshirt pocket and said, "We'll pick up Arnold Bakers first."

I noticed that he wasn't twitching today. I asked if he took his medicine. He cocked his head and chuckled. "Huh, are ya worried?"

"Uh, I ain't worried Nutsey. Just saying."

Nutsey rested his head back on the seat and lit another cigarette.

Just then Dana called.

"Frank, this is Dana." Needless to say she was distraught, and in tears. She muttered, "What am I going to do?"

I told her that I couldn't talk now. Dana was breathing heavy. She paused for a second, "I'm sorry for calling. I realize that you're with Nutsey, but I need to know that you're getting closer to finding out who's behind all of this?"

My conversation was guarded, so I could only reply, "No, I'm not."

Dana let out a long sigh. "Oh-----."

Nutsey was listening to my every word.

My cell phone began to beep. I told Dana that I had to take another call. "Hello."

It was Howell. Again my conversation was guarded. "Friedman just woke me up. New Rochelle PD called him about the truck being torched. Is there anything you can add?"

"No nothing."

All that the prick wanted to know was if I could add anything, so he could brief Hogan. Howell should have known that I couldn't talk. He should have realized that Nutsey was sitting next to me. Undaunted, I squawked back, "It's not a good time. I gotta go," and hung up.

Before I could put the phone away, it rang again. This time it was Nulligan. I saw that Nutsey was antsy and wanted me to hurry. He anxiously lit another cigarette; the smoke curled upward filling the cab, making it hard for me to breathe.

"Nutsey, I got a call. Please roll down the window."

He shot me a hard look and replied, "You're a popular guy, but we got garbage to pick up."

Nulligan, unlike Howell, knew I couldn't talk and said that Howell got him out of bed to pump me about the fire. "Frankie, I know you can't talk now, so call me later."

Arnold Bakers is right off I-95, at exit two, on the Connecticut line. I drove into the bakery as Nutsey pointed to the back of the building. There it was a 150 yarder by the back entrance. I connected on my first try, unloading it without a problem. I was becoming good at this job, but still hoping that the bad guys would try to pull the truck over and try to do something stupid. What a surprise they would get.

The rest of the stops in Greenwich also went great and we continued on our regular route into Rye and Port Chester. At 11:30 A.M., we stopped at Nutsey's favorite coffee shop, on Midland Avenue in Rye. While Nutsey went into buy coffee and bagels, I shot Nulligan a call. "Hey Joe, I don't have much time, but I can talk now."

"Sure. Howell wants to know if there is any additional information about the torch job."

"No. Only that someone is trying to put Dana out of business." I told Joe that I felt like I was just spinning my wheels driving the truck. Nothing was happening. No threats, no attempted assaults, no nothing.

"Ah well, buddy, you've only been at it less than a week. Give it some time."

"Joe, driving the truck is killing me. I've got to take a drink just to get behind the wheel."

Joe laughed. "Hang in there buddy."

"Oh, by the way, before I forget, the other night I was followed and then chased into the Bronx. If they didn't hit two parked cars, I think, I'd have had a problem."

"Did you get a look at them?"

"No, but they'll need a new ride." Nutsey walked out of the store with coffee and buttered rolls. "Joe, Nutsey's coming. I gotta go."

"Okay, Frankie. But before you hang up, My informant got a lead on Crazy Alex."

"Okay, I'll talk to you soon."

Nutsey climbed up into the cab. He took a bite of his buttered roll and a sip of coffee, and with a mouthful, mumbled, "We'd better dump the load, before we pick up at the Rye Grill."

"Sounds like a plan, Nutsey."

After dumping at the transfer station, the rest of the day went as smooth as silk. I'm sure that a few hits of Cognac took the edge off and relaxed me. We finished up and got back to the yard at about 4:30 P.M. Newcomb's car was in the yard and he was probably up in the office. I wanted to make a quick exit, so I fueled the truck, parked it in the garage, and quickly left.

CHAPTER THIRTEEN

I told Denise about Tommy being shot by a thug who tried to extort him
into letting him work out at his gym free of charge. Now, Tommy and his
family are hiding at his mother-in-law's because the creep found out
where he lived in Riverdale. Needless to say, Denise was very upset, and
it has kept her awake a few nights.

It was Saturday morning and Denise and I were still in bed sleeping when
my cell phone rang. Half asleep, I answered, "Hello."

"Franco."

"Good morning ma. What time is it?"

"Sono le nove."

A little annoyed, I answered curtly. "Ma, I'm awake now. Please speak
English."

Denise face down on the pillow, mumbled, "Uh, who is it?"

"It's my mother."

In a gentle voice, speaking in broken English, she said that she had talked
to Helen and if I wasn't working tomorrow, I could pick up Catie and
Francesca. Ma was making manicotti.

This was music to my ears. "Ma, that's great! What time?"

"Twelve - a."

"Okay ma. See you tomorrow."

Yawning, I reached over, put my phone back on the night stand, and sat
up. Denise was now awake. I guess by the look on my face she could tell
I was happy. She sat up, placing her hand on the back of my neck, gently
rubbing it. "What's going on?"

"I'm picking the girls up tomorrow. My mother's cooking. My brother and Barbara are coming."

Denise smiled. "That's great! I'll finally get to meet your family."

We lay back down, embracing one another. Denise kissed my lips and whispered, "I'm so happy we're together."

I held her by the waist, pulling her tightly against my body. I kissed her face and mouth. We could hardly breathe. My voice gentle and reflective, I said, "I love you." We made love and at that moment felt closer than ever.

After lying there for a while Denise said, "I'll make coffee. I'm so excited to finally meet your mom!"

I lay on back on the bed with my hands cupped behind my head and mouthed, "I'm glad that you're gonna meet her too, sexy."

Denise made breakfast and we ate in the dining area, talking about what my family was like and her job at Shell Oil. She was doing well and was up for a raise. She loved her job and said that her company is in the process of obtaining permits from the US Government to drill off the Alaskan coast. She said that our government is slow in issuing permits because of environmental issues. They don't want another oil spill to ruin the eco system and the industries attached to it. It would be a financial disaster for all concerned. She said that when the permits are issued, there's a good chance she'd be going to Alaska for a few weeks to identify the drilling sites.

I was off, and this would be her first Sunday at my mother's house, and hopefully not the last. The excitement of meeting Catie and Francesca resonated in her voice. She was reluctant to bring up our trip to Providence and Tommy being shot, but she did. With a slight frown she said, "Do you think that you'll ever do anything else to earn a living?"

Puzzled, I asked, "Why?"

"Because I'm afraid you'll be killed!"

"It's what I do."

She stared at me, nervously curling a few strands of hair around her forefinger as she looked down into her coffee cup.

"Look Denise, I was born to be a cop, and I love the job. There's nothing else I want to do."

Denise continued eating her toast and didn't say anything more about it. For the rest of the day we sat around listening to soft rock and reading the local newspapers. About 3:30 P.M., we went into the bedroom and turned on the TV to watch a movie. *Scar Face* was about to start on HBO. We planned to stay in for the rest of the night and order a thin crusted pizza from our favorite pizza place. Wine wasn't a problem; I had a few bottles in the hall closet.

We were on the go all week. For me, there was nothing better than staying home, kicking back with a few glasses of wine, and watching a good movie. We'd just finished eating the last two slices of pizza when my cell phone rang. Nulligan called. "Hey Joe, what's up?"

Joe was excited. He said that his C.I. had found out that Shivone's staying at the Roger Smith Hotel in White Plains.

"Joe, that's great. Let's check it out tonight. Can Angel work?" I looked over at Denise who was listening. "Joe, that's a section eight, welfare hotel."

"Pisano told my C.I. that Alex had recently checked into the hotel under the assumed name, Danny Patti."

By now, Denise had lowered the sound on the TV. Disappointment was written all over her face.

"Okay, what time and where do you want to meet up?"

"Angel and I will meet you on the corner of Chestnut and Maple, at 11:45 P.M."

Barely able to control her displeasure, Denise said curtly, "So… do you have to go?"

I reached for her hand. "I have to work tonight. We found out where Shivone is hiding."

She looked concerned. "Oh, what's that mean?"

"It means I'm gonna lock him up."

The rest of the evening we hardly spoke. She pretended to watch the end of the movie, but I knew that she was upset that I had to leave. But I guess she was more concerned about my well being.

I remember that night like it was yesterday. As a matter of fact, I'll never forget what happened. The air was cool for the end of June. I jumped on the Bronx River Parkway and headed for White Plains, parking on Chestnut Street. The Roger Smith Hotel was on the corner of Chestnut and East Post Road. I looked around for Angel and Joe. They hadn't arrived yet. I walked up to the opposite corner and waited. It was a quiet night, except for the occasional car that passed by. Shortly, Joe and Angel pulled up. Joe parked his car as short distance from where I was standing.

Joe was wired. "I got Alex's picture. We'll show it to the night clerk and see if he knows him." Joe pulled out the photo and showed it to me and Angel.

Joe continued, "My informant said that Alex is armed. We gotta be careful."

Angel, impatient to get a move on it, sounded off. "Frankie, you ready?"

"Yeah Angel, I'm ready to make a move, but I want to make sure that we're on solid ground. "Uh, anybody got a copy of the warrant?"

Angel pulled the warrant from his jacket pocket and opened it. "Yo, its right here."

I closed my fist, giving a thumbs up. "Okay, let's rock and roll."

We slowly walked into the hotel. The hotel was run down, dark and depressing. Ugly plastic potted Palm trees were placed around the lobby. The elevator was to the right of the front desk. Its doors were all banged up from the constant use. I know that it's a welfare hotel, but they could have spruced up the place a little so that the residents don't feel like committing suicide. The lobby was dimly lit. The night clerk, an Asian man in his late fifties, looked a little worn for wear. He was wearing a black cardigan sweater that had holes at the elbows. His navy blue slacks were dirty and wrinkled. As we walked in, he was reading the late edition of the New York Post.

He shot straight up when he realized that we were standing in front of him. His face was twisted, as he looked over his glasses. In a strained voice he said, "Can I help you?"

Joe took out his shield, sticking it in the guys face. "Police, we're looking for Alex Shivone, he sometimes uses the name Danny Patti." He took out Alex's mug shot, throwing it down on the desk in front of him. "Is he staying here?"

The clerk paused for a second then nodded yes. "You just missed him. He walked in a few minutes ago and took the elevator up to his room."

In his textured Spanish accent, Angel asked, "What's his room number?"

The clerk fumbling with the newspaper, squealed, "He's in room 501."

I barked, "Yo, give us the pass key."

The clerk reluctantly turned around and opened a cache of drawers in a wooden rack behind the desk. He took out a ring of keys, removed a key tagged, room 501, and handed it to Angel. Joe reached over, grabbed the clerk, and pulled him over the desk by his neck. They were nose to nose. In a menacing voice Joe said, "Don't think about picking up the phone, and tipping him off. I can be your worst fucking nightmare." Joe slowly let go of him and pushed him back across the desk.

The clerk was obviously frightened, and nodded that he understood. His eyes followed us to the elevator, as Joe pushed the up button. We stepped into the elevator taking it to the fifth floor. Not a word was said on the ride up. We glanced at each other from time to time, but remained mute.

Room 501 was directly across the hall from the elevator. I don't know about Joe and Angel, but my adrenalin was pumping. Every man knows fear, managing it is the hard part. We drew our weapons as Angel slid the key into the lock. With one hand he grabbed the door knob and with the other, he quietly pushed the door open. Joe and I rushed into the dimly lit one room suite. Mind you, this happened in a matter of seconds. We passed a bathroom on our right, yelling, "Police, police!"

Our senses were sharp. Our eyes darted around the room looking for Alex, but he wasn't there. His wallet and car keys were lying on an old beat up dresser. There was an open suitcase filled with crumpled clothes sitting on the end of the bed. I even looked under the bed. We noticed a glimmer of light from under the bathroom door. Joe tried the door knob. It was locked. He yelled out, "Alex, police," and threw his shoulder full force into the door. The door shook to its frame. With a burst of energy, he reared back and slammed his body into the door. This time it exploded, almost knocking it off its hinges.

There he was. His treacherous brown eyes stared up at us as he cowered naked on the floor between the shower stall and the toilet holding a gun. Joe had his pistol at the ready. He shouted at the top of his lungs, "Alex, drop the gun, you're under arrest!"

Angel and I were almost on top of Joe. What I'm about to tell you isn't for the weak of heart. Things were happening so fast. It was surreal. Mayhem was about to ensue in that tiny bathroom. I screamed, "Alex, drop the fucking gun! Drop the gun!" Alex raised a twenty-five caliber automatic pistol directly at us and fired. I heard the bullet whizz by my head, ripping into the wall behind me. I reacted and fired three times. Bang, bang, bang, hitting him once in the torso. It didn't put him down. Alex was about to squeeze off another round when Joe fired, putting a .45

caliber round just above his right eye. It blew half of his skull away. Brain matter, blood and bone fragments sprayed all over us. I knew he was dead, but his nervous system continued to react. He wretched, gurgled, and twitched with only half a head. They say that the human body holds up to ten pints of blood, well I can believe it. There was so much blood on the floor and the walls it going to take crime scene cleaners hours to clean up the mess.

Gun smoke filled the bathroom, circling the overhead light, as a reminder of what had just taken place. We stood there stunned, staring down at Alex's corpse, realizing that a human life had just been taken. Now we had to deal with the emotional fallout. Joe turned to me and Angel with a sense of urgency. "We have to call this in."

Angel stood quietly. There was no need to say anything. Alex Shivone was dead. Joe took out his cell phone and called the White Plains PD. Then he shot a call into Acting Chief Howell. Howell didn't ask how he was holding up. All that he was wanted to know if the shooting was a righteous shooting.

In a matter of minutes, sirens were heard off in the distance. The PD would arrive soon. Alex's days of intimating people, and his life of crime had come to a tragic end.

His body was carried out through the lobby on a gurney by people from the Medical Examiners Office. The night clerk watched as we walked out of the hotel into the night. It wasn't until 3:30 A.M. when I finally arrived home. Denise was asleep on the living room couch with the lights on. I tiptoed into the kitchen, took a tumbler from the kitchen cabinet, grabbed the bottle of Cognac off the counter, and poured a stiff drink. I guess the sound of the bottle hitting the glass woke her up. She said something as she awoke from a deep sleep. "Frankie, is that you? Are you okay?"

I threw back the cognac in one swallow and managed to get the words out. "Yeah, babe, I'm fine. Let's go to bed."

Still drowsy, she got up from the couch and walked into the kitchen. Apparently some of Alex's blood was on my sweatshirt. Denise couldn't help but notice it. She stood there glaring at me. "Where'd the blood come from? Whose blood is it?"

"I can't talk about right now. Let's just say it's a night I'd like to forget ever happened."

Denise's face turned red under the overhead light in the kitchen. She asked, "Is it Shivone's blood?"

"Yes, it's his blood. We had to kill him tonight. Please understand that I don't want to talk about it right now."

She wrapped her arms around me and kissed my cheek. "I'm so sorry for you. I don't know what else to say."

"There's nothing to say."

We walked into the bedroom, and got into bed. She fell asleep right away, but I wasn't so lucky. I stared up at the ceiling most of the night, trying not to think about Alex's face. It was useless. Ghostlike flashbacks of Alex lying there gurgling haunted me all night.

In a few hours Denise would be meeting my kids, and the rest of my family. I wasn't sure that I could handle leaving my apartment, much less visit my mother. The shooting caused such a fire storm that it twisted my insides around so badly that I couldn't think straight.

Thank God it was Sunday morning and I could finally get on with the day.

CHAPTER FOURTEEN

The front door of the brick faced duplex on Allerton Avenue in the Bronx slowly opened. We waited on the sidewalk next to Denise's car. Catie, holding her doll, and Francesca carrying Catie's car seat, ran out of the house shouting, "Daddy, Daddy". Francesca put the car seat down and jumped up into my arms. Catie grabbed my legs, her momentum almost knocking me to the ground. Catie looked like the smaller version of her mother. She's four years old, barely three feet tall. She has her mother's silky white complexion, blond hair, and lovely blue eyes. Francesca's seven and looks like my clone. She's tall for her age, small boned like me, with dark brown hair.

Helen peered curiously though the living room blinds wanting to get a glimpse of Denise.

"Hi, I'm Denise. It's so nice to meet the both of you."

Francesca shyly said, "Hi, I'm Francesca," as Catie stood there anxiously holding her doll. Francesca, bright eyed, looked up and asked, "Daddy, are we going to grandma's?"

"Yes, sweetheart. Now take your sisters hand and let's get in the car. Grandma is waiting for us."

Denise took hold of the car seat and helped the girls into the back seat. I walked around to the driver's side and climbed in. Of course, the girls wanted to know how long it would take to get to grandma's house. Driving on I-95, it was only a few miles to the Harrison exit. My mother lives in the Franklin Park section of Harrison. I've mentioned that my grandfather has lived with my mother since my dad passed away. He's in his mid-eighties, spry as a rooster, and speaks very little English.

On the drive up, Denise and I made small talk, while Catie played with her doll and Francesca looked at Denise, trying to figure her out. Sensing that Francesca was uncomfortable, Denise turned around to reassure her. "Hey Francesca, are you okay?"

Francesca timidly began to speak. She came out with something that literally stunned the both of us. "Daddy", she paused, as if she really didn't want to say what she was thinking. "Mommy says that you're just like the bad people you put in jail. Is that true?"

Denise's jaw dropped. She turned around, placing her hand on Francesca's cheek, softly stroking it and said, "No darling, that's not true, your Daddy is a good man."

Francesca lowered her head as if she'd said something wrong. Denise looked at me shaking her head, as if she wanted to say, what a thing to tell your child about their father. I didn't say anything. All I could think about was last night and all the other nights like it. Only now, Denise is in my life, and trying to handle what Helen couldn't.

When I first met Denise, I told her that I never talked with Helen about my job. For the most part, the cases I worked were classified as confidential. I promised Denise that I would talk about my work as much as I could, but last night, I just couldn't bring myself to talk about the shooting. The words just wouldn't come out.

I looked into the rear view mirror and got a candid peak at my girls. As I looked at them, I was thinking that my divorce from Helen has affected them in a big way. After all, Helen and I were their foundation, their rock. They were innocent kids caught up in an adult mess. I can't be selfish anymore. I need to make them my priority in life. They've got to know that they can count on me. Maybe it's time for me to opt out of undercover assignments. I'll just have to see how things play out in the next few months.

What happened in Providence upset Denise. It gave her a bird's eye view into the world I live in. I know that she loves me, but is her love strong enough to hold us together? I don't want another failed relationship. I don't want to lose her. Denise sensed that I'd slipped away into another place. She looked over, gently touching my shoulder, whispering, "Frankie, you with me? You seem to be somewhere else."

"Sorry, I was just daydreaming."

Denise slid closer. "Don't let anything get in the way of your spending the day with your girls."

"I won't."

I pointed out my grammar school, Parsons Memorial, as we passed it on Halstead Avenue. I turned onto Franklin Avenue and saw my grandfather standing in front of the house, smoking a De Nobili cigar, his favorite. He, like many Italian-Americans who immigrated from Italy, favored the De Nobili. It's made of the finest Tennessee and Kentucky dark fired tobacco and a dried curing process gives it a distinctive flavor which my grandfather loves. There he was puffing away as I pulled up. My grandfather never expressed much emotion. He reinforced my parent's edicts and always said that a man's word is his bond. You don't need a legal contract to get things done. All that was necessary was an honest handshake. My grandfather is a proud man, who speaks very little English. He stands 5'7" and weighs 150 pounds soaking wet, but he's tough as nails. He usually dresses in a suit and tie. Perhaps it gives him a sense of self-respect. He's well known in the town for his signature fedora hat, and having a copy of 'Il Progresso', the Italian language newspaper, under his arm. He loves going to the Harrison Italian-American Club, where he debates politics and religion with other members. He's also an avid reader, although he's never had the opportunity for a formal education. His quest for knowledge is unyielding. His personal library hosts hundreds of books, many by great Italian philosophers like Renaissance philosopher Bernardino Telesio, and 20th century Italian philosopher Benedetto Croce.

Denise could hardly wait to get the party started. She quickly opened the car door, releasing the latch on the front seat, letting the girls out. I yelled, "Girls, make sure that you say hello to your Great Grandfather, Grande Nonno."

Francesca and Catie ran up to him, giving him a big hug. "Hi Nonno," they shouted affectionately.

He tenderly reached down, patting the top of their heads. "Caio bella Francesca, ciao bella Catarina."

I joined him on the sidewalk, embracing him, and kissed him on the cheek and said "Ciao, Nonno."

It's a tradition that Italian men kiss one another to show their love. With a gleam in his eye he said, "Franco, e bello ci vediamo e Francesca e Catarina. Per favore, presenta io a la ragazza." I looked at Denise. My grandfather said how pretty Francesca and Catie are and asked me to introduce you to him. He extended his hand his hand to Denise, and if I know my grandfather, he gave her the once over.

"Denise, I'd like you to meet my grandfather, Guarino."

She reached out taking his hand. "I'm so happy to meet you Mr. Grossi, Frankie has told me so much about you."

I knew by the way he looked at her that he liked her. He slowly released her hand, smiling. "Bella ragazza, senorella."

She looked at me if she wanted me to translate. "He said that you're a pretty girl."

Her face lit up, blushing as she smiled, and asked me how to say thank you in Italian.

I looked over grinning, "It's *grazie.*"

"*Grazie,* Mr. Grossi."

My grandfather turned toward the house and in his Italian language said that my brother and Barbara were already here. I asked if he was coming in. He loved to speak in his rhythmic Italian and said, "Prima io fine il sigaro. Vieni a casa."

Denise raised her eyebrows, shrugging her shoulders. I knew that she wanted me to translate. "He said that he'd be in after he finishes his cigar." The girls were giggling, as I reached over and stretched out my arm, wrapping them around their shoulders. "Let's go girls. Nonno will be in soon."

We all walked up the front steps. Before I had a chance to ring the doorbell, Richie opened the door. With an enormous grin, he said, "Well, hello brother! This must be Denise. Hi Denise, I'm Rich, it's nice to finally meet you." Then he playfully reached out to greet the girls. "Hi Catie, hi Francesca, give Uncle Richie a big hug."

The girls gave him a hug and said, "Hi Uncle Richie," and ran past him into the living room.

Richie took Denise's hand grinning from ear to ear and said, "Welcome! You're beautiful. My brother said that you were."

She blushed. "Thank you, Richie."

We walked in and I told my brother that I was disappointed that his boys weren't here. He replied, "I know. My mother-in law had tickets to a Broadway show. They're seeing Chitty Chitty Bang Bang."

The smell of frying meatballs and sausages filled the house. Denise looked at me and back at my brother, smiling. "Frankie, I've never smelled anything like it. The aroma is wonderful." Denise looked at me and said, "I can't believe how much you guys look alike."

Richie replied, "Denise, the only difference between my brother and me is that I dress on the conservative side and, as you can see, and I have no mustache."

My mother and Barbara must have heard us talking and walked into the living room. When Francesca and Catie saw my mother, their faces lit up and they cried out as they ran to her. "Nonni! Nonni!"

She bent down, embracing them. She stood there, caressing their faces, and said in Italian, "Mia cuore Francesca e Catarina."

Denise looked as if she were about to cry, and sighed, "Oh..., Frankie, please tell me what your mother just said."

"My mother said that Catie and Francesca are her heart."

Barbara was beaming from ear to ear. Her hazel eyes caught the sunlight as she stood there. "Hi, Denise. I'm Barbara. Glad to meet you." Barbara reached over and kissed her on the cheek.

Denise said graciously, "It's nice to meet you too."

Like my grandfather, my mother was giving Denise the once over before walking over and taking hold of both of her hands. "Bella senorella. Denise, is a- so beautiful."

Denise was at a loss for words for a moment. "Thank you, Mrs. Santorsola."

Barbara and my brother have been married for ten years and as I've mentioned have three boys. My mother, skilled at the art of making us feel guilty, complains about us not having more grandchildren. She's constantly mentioning that our father came from a family of thirteen. He had seven sisters and six brothers. Our typical response is, "Yeah Ma, we know, but this is the twenty first century."

Barbara was excited. She took Denise by the hand and they walked into the hallway. "Let me show you the rest of house. We'll start with the bedrooms upstairs."

My grandfather came in and asked my brother to bring up a few bottles of homemade wine from the basement. My mother took hold of Catie and Francesca and walked into the kitchen followed by my grandfather. Richie brought the wine into the dining room. He and I then settled in to catch up with each other's lives. As I was speaking to my brother, I could hear Catie and Francesca laughing, as my mother spoke to them. Richie asked, "It was in the morning newspaper. Shivone was killed last night."

"Yeah, I know, I was there." My mind raced a hundred miles an hour. Breathing hard, I said, "Huh, I don't want to talk about it. I don't want to have to live with it today." I placed my index finger to my lips, as if to say be quiet, then pointing to the kitchen and to the floor above. "You got it?"

Richie looked over as if trying to get a read on my thoughts. "Are you alright?"

I began to tense up from all the questions. "Richie, like I said, I don't want to talk about."

"Frankie, I'm your brother."

"Rich, I'm okay. The fucking guy was trying to kill our Cousin Tommy. We had no choice. I just want to keep a lid on it for today."

Richie was undoubtedly upset. He was frustrated with the kind of police work I was doing. It was written all over his face. He raised his voice and said, "Try not blowing it with Denise! Rethink this undercover bullshit! And start thinking about your future, brother!"

Denise and Barbara walked in. Barbara asked, "What's all the commotion about? Are you guys arguing?"

I gave her a wink. "Barb, we're not arguing. We're just talking." My little girls ran into the living room laughing. They jumped on my lap giggling, playfully wrapping their arms around my neck. Francesca looked up at me grinning. "Nonni said we'll eat in a little while."

I smiled into her eyes that seem to sparkle and said, "Okay sweetie."

I'll never forget how Denise lit up that day. Her lips curled upward as she smiled, lighting up her face. She said excitedly, "Frankie, Richie brought a few bottles of homemade wine from the basement, can you show me the wine cellar?"

"Sure."

I got up, gently nudging the girls off my lap. "Sure, honey." Anything was better than talking about last night. "Girls, hang out with your uncle and aunt for a while. I'm going to show Denise Nonno's wine cellar."

Denise and I walked down the hallway to the old wooden cellar door. As we walked down the steps, I could hear my mother laughing about something that my grandfather said. I heard her say, "Papa, please take it easy with the wine. The day is young."

I can't tell you how many times I've walked up and down these stairs, lugging homemade wine up from the basement. My father and grandfather drank it at every meal. Wine making has been a part of our family tradition since my grandfather, at twenty five years of age, immigrated from Rimini, a small town in Northern Italy. When he arrived in America, he was ready to see the streets paved with gold.

I flipped on the light switch at the top of the stairs. A 150 watt light bulb hung at the bottom of the stairs. Much to Denise's surprise, it looked like a modern day winery. My grandfather, as old as he is, had just painted the walls white, and the floors grey. Hugging the wall at the bottom of the stairs was a small maple dresser, used to store some of the wine equipment and the chemicals used in the wine making process. On top of the table sat a test tube for testing the potential alcohol level of the wine. There were beakers for mixing and air locks to let the carbon dioxide escape from the fermenting barrels, preventing air from getting in and spoiling the fermenting wine. French oak aging barrels lined the walls.

Her voice full of excitement, "Huh, I can't believe this! This is awesome! You have to tell me how you make wine."

The girls came running down the stairs and said, "Daddy, Daddy, grandma said to come up in ten minutes. We're ready to eat."

The girls ran past us giggling, exploring all of the wine making equipment. They've watched me press the grapes into wine a few times. As I was explaining the procedure to Denise, I notice that her mood seemed to change. I felt it, something was wrong. I guess that deep down inside I knew what it was. Providence was an eye opener for her and now naturally she was having a problem with the Shivone shooting. I decided not to say anything, for now, it was better to let things go and not spoil the day. I went on to explain the wine making process that my grandfather taught us. Denise was mesmerized by what she was hearing. She looked at me dumbstruck. "Frankie, I'm in awe."

I asked if she'd like to help next time we make wine. She smiled and said that she would love to. The girls overheard me, and asked if they could help too. Then they ran up the stairs.

Denise threw her arms around me, tilting her head back slightly, smiling. "Wow! I'm impressed! I love the sensitive side of you."

I felt that this was the perfect time to broach the subject, since she had opened the door. "Well," I asked, "How about the insensitive side of me? Do you love me enough to deal with my job? Now that you've met my family, especially Catie and Francesca, are you willing accept the whole package?"

Her eyes welled up, as she pushed away from me. She looked directly into my eyes. "I've given you every part of me. I love you with all my heart, but I truly don't know if I can bear the intensity of your work, and what it does to you. Let's give it some time. I want us to be together more than anything in the world."

I felt like I'd been hit in the stomach with a two by four. I should have expected this. Thoughts of us tumbled through my mind. I felt taken aback after her profession of her love. It was hard for me to say anything. I stood there speechless.

Footsteps were heard at the top of the stairs. Barbara's voice echoed down. "Dinner's ready!"

We stared silently at each other for a moment, realizing the gravity of what had just been said. I reached for Denise's hand, barely able to contain my feelings. "We'd better go up."

We slowly walked up the stairs and into the dining room. Everyone was seated at the table. I guess they could feel that something was wrong. The room suddenly became quiet and all eyes were on us. The tension in the air was so thick you could cut it with a knife. My mother immediately asked if I was feeling okay. Looking a bit dejected, I looked at her and replied, "Yeah, ma. Everything is fine."

My grandfather sat at the head of the table. It's an Italian tradition that the oldest family member sits at the head of the table. My mother on the other hand, was sitting at the far end of the table in easy reach of the freshly prepared food. Naturally, the girls sat on each side of her. Denise's mood lightened and she commented on how lovely the table looked. "Mrs. Santorsola, the table setting is beautiful, and the smell of the manicotti is making my mouth water. I can't wait to start eating. She turned to my grandfather smiling. "Mr. Grossi, I also can't wait to try your homemade wine. I'm sure it's going to be delicious." He looked back at her smiling, and nodding his head in approval.

There were two bottles of wine on the table in front of my grandfather. He already had one open. My mom told him again to go easy. He just looked at her, filled his glass, and then passed the bottle around the table. And, in Italian said, "Tuti mangare la familia." Which means, "Everybody in the family eat."

My mother stood, asking that the dishes be passed to her so she could fill them. I looked over at Denise as she lifted her glass and took a sip of red wine. She looked over at my grandfather with a gleam in her eye, and said, "Mr. Grossi, this is delicious."

Francesca and Catie sat there enjoying the manicotti and drinking Shirley Temples. They were finished in no time and asked to leave the table to watch TV. I told them that they were excused. Everyone at the table was enjoying my mother's home cooking. I was glad to see Denise savoring every morsel of food. She swallowed a mouthful, trying to speak as she mumbled, "This is delicious."

Barbara blurted out, "Frankie, Tommy and Anna must be so relieved to know that Shivone is finally out of their life."

"Yeah, everyone is relieved. The guy was a menace to society. I'm glad the animal is dead."

My mother asked, "Figlio Mio. Va Tutto bene?"

"Yeah, ma. I'm fine. Let's talk about happier things."

Denise looked like she was uncomfortable and began to fidget in her chair. My brother quickly changed the subject. Our conversation centered on my mother's cooking, our childhood memories, and our careers. After dinner, my mother served a homemade cheesecake and coffee.

My grandfather took a bottle of Anisette and cordial glasses from the curio cabinet behind him. He loved to serve Anisette as an after dinner drink. It's a clear liquor made from the anise plant. It has a licorice flavor. Nonno likes it straight, but my mother likes it cloudy, so she dilutes it with water. It changes from clear to cloudy, when water is added. Denise tried it, and loved it.

We all helped with the dishes, something that my brother and I don't like to do. But, we sucked it up and helped anyway. It was getting late, and I had to get the girls home. Denise thanked my mother for a wonderful dinner and told everyone how glad she was to meet them as we left.

There wasn't much conversation on our way to drop off the kids. But, as soon as they were out of the car, Denise's attitude changed. She seemed distant. She started to cry. She wiped away the tears and said, "I know you have a lot of pent up emotions that you can't share. I don't know how to comfort you? I wish I did."

There was nothing I could say. She knew what my life was all about going into our relationship.

CHAPTER FIFTEEN

I didn't sleep that night. I couldn't stop thinking about the shooting. The next day, Nutsey noticed that I wasn't myself and asked if I had something on my mind. I lied and said that I was fine. But the truth of it was, the thought of loosing Denise turned my world upside down.

I remember the day being hot and humid when we unloaded the container at George's Pharmacy in Rye. After the stop, we headed to the Town & County Coffee Shop to grab a coffee. Nutsey said that he'd get a jump on it and cut through the vacant lot next to the coffee shop. I pulled around the block, rounding the corner, and noticed a small blue hatchback parked in front of the store. A delivery man got out of the car and opened the back, removing what looked like boxes of pastries. He carried them into the store. I remember slowing the truck down, as I neared the shop. I hit the air brakes, but nothing happened. The brake pedal had no resistance and plummeted to the floor board. I took a deep breath and hit the brakes again. I hit the fucking thing so hard I almost sent my foot through the floor board. I knew it was all over but the shouting. I started to gasp for air. I was so scared my heart was pounding so loud that it hurt my fucking eardrums. I was now breathing in short repetitive bursts. The truck was only about twenty feet from the compact car and gaining. I didn't have to be psychic to see what was coming next. It was inevitable. Suddenly, I surrendered to the moment, throwing my head back against the seat, I closed my eyes, and screamed, "Oh God, oh my God! Please, I can't take this anymore! " I'm sure they heard me up the street. Moments later, there was a loud bang and the sound of crunching metal as the truck slammed into the small hatchback. I opened my eyes and the next thing I see is the little blue car, the size of an accordion, about one hundred feet up the street. The garbage truck was now resting in front of the store.

I just sat there for a minute thinking how fucked I was. I knew I had to call Newcomb and give them the bad news. I also knew that there was no way I'd be rolling around in the dirt with him again. I slowly gained my composure and got out of the truck. I looked around to see if anyone witnessed the accident. Apparently, no one had. I walked into the store. The counterman glared at me, but Nutsey didn't say anything. He stood nonchalantly at the counter with his head down. I thought, how strange,

Nutsey's not flipping out. How could he not have heard the crash? It was baffling to me. My head was spinning as I slowly walked up to him. I leaned in and whispered in his ear, "Nutsey, I hit the car."

Nutsey turned to me calmly, pretending for a split second that he didn't see the accident. Then he piped up, swearing under his breath and said, "Uh, I know. I know you hit the fucking car."

Just then, the delivery guy, a short Hispanic guy in his mid-thirties, walked out of the back room holding an invoice. He immediately saw the garbage truck parked where his car was parked. He began screaming. "What the fuck! My car, my car!" He threw the invoice into the air, and ran past us like the devil was chasing him. He stood screaming in front of the store, looking up the street at what was left of his car. "Oh my God! My fucking car! Look what you did to my car!"

The counterman stood there mute. Nutsey calmly shrugged his shoulders, and said, "Uh, I guess you'd better call Shorty."

In shock, I gritted my teeth and replied, "I guess I better." In the meantime, the delivery man ran back into the store, yelling, "Look what you did to my fucking car!"

I figured that I'd better go on the offensive with this guy. "Calm down. My company's insurance will take care of your car. Don't worry about it."

He made a wrenching sound, then howled, "Don't worry about it? What do I do in the meantime, don't worry about it? I need a car!" He ran back into the back room, hollering that he had to call his insurance agent.

Nutsey went out to check the brakes on the truck, while the counter man stood there with his mouth open. Reluctantly, I took out my cell phone and punched in the office number, but there was no answer. I left a short message on the answering machine that my brakes failed and I that I had a slight accident. It wasn't thirty seconds and my phone rang. It was Newcomb. His high-pitched voice echoed through the phone so loudly that I had to pull it away from my ear. "Only you, Miranda! Why does everything have to happen to you?"

"Hey, it wasn't my fault. The fucking brakes failed."

He asked if the truck was drivable.

"No. It'll have to be towed."

"Okay, Miranda. I'll send a tow truck."

I quickly scribbled the office number on a piece of paper and handed it to the delivery man, who was now walking around in circles mumbling to himself. Nutsey and I walked out of the store, climbed back into the truck, and waited for the tow truck to arrive. A late model black Cadillac Sedan pulled up a few feet in front of the truck and stopped. I wasn't thinking, my mind was on the accident, and didn't realize that this was the moment I'd been waiting for. The doors of the sedan flew open and two guys jumped out. That's when I snapped out of it. I looked at Nutsey who looked like he was about to shit himself.

One guy, a ruddy looking Italian guy, started for the truck and said, "Hey, we want to talk to you." The skinny light skinned guy, stood by the trunk of the Cadillac.

I yelled to Nutsey to stay in the truck and I jumped out. I figured that these are the guys who are intimidating and assaulting the drivers. I was right. The guy walking towards me pulled out a blackjack and raised it at me. I jumped back, pulled out my 9 millimeter, and told him to freeze. All I remember is the guy stopping in his tracks, and the skinny guy pulling out a gun and opening up on me. I heard the sound of his bullets as they whizzed by. I was wired and aware of every sound and movement around me. Suddenly, time and motion stood still. I felt like I was viewing a movie, one frame at a time. Maybe I imagined it, but I saw the muzzle flashes from his gun as he continued to fire at me. It was surreal. I don't know how I wasn't shot. Somehow, I managed to squeeze off a few rounds. I heard the skinny guy scream, "I'm hit!"

Then suddenly time and motion kicked back in. They both turned and ran back into the car. The skinny one was holding his shoulder. Before I had a chance to fire more rounds off, the driver slammed the car into gear, burning rubber as he sped down the road. I turned back to look at Nutsey. Two bullets had pierced the windshield, shattering it. Nutsey was slumped to his side, his body resting on the steering wheel. I ran over to him. His eyes were closed. He'd been shot. I quickly jumped up onto the running board, pulled opened the door, and leaned in. His overalls were blood soaked. He was unconscious, and moaning. But at least he was breathing. I lifted him out of the truck and tore his overalls down to his waist, ripping open his shirt. There was a gaping hole under his left collar bone. A steady stream of blood was spewing from the wound. All I could think of was Nutsey might die. I felt responsible. I quickly applied pressure to the wound, using the palm of my hand to stem the bleeding. I shoved some of his undershirt into the wound, causing a bloodcurdling scream from him. I didn't have time for emotions. I had to react, using the first aid training I'd received in the police academy. In what seemed like an eternity, I heard sirens off in the distance.

Nutsey opened his eyes for a moment, but they shut again. The adrenalin pumped through me. Soon three police cruisers from the City of Rye PD arrived. I slipped the 9 millimeter back into my pants, so I wouldn't be shot. As an ambulance pulled up, two uniformed cops ran up to me, threw me against the side of the truck, searched, and cuffed me for their safety. They didn't know if I was the shooter. They discovered the 9mm and confiscated it. Once I was secured, EMS personnel began administering first aid. They gave Nutsey pure oxygen and a blood transfusion. The uniformed sergeant at the scene asked me my name and if I knew who shot Nutsey. I had no choice, I had to identify myself. I told him that I worked for the District Attorneys Office, working undercover, on the garbage truck. I said that acting Chief John Howell will verify who I am. I advised the sergeant that I shot one of the perpetrators. One of the cops pulled out my wallet, removed my fictitious driver's license, and handed it to the sergeant. Sergeant Shkreli glanced at my license for a second and asked me for my chief's direct number, and proceeded to call him. Howell confirmed that I was an undercover cop investigating the trio of homicides. After their brief conversation, he directed a patrolman to remove the handcuffs.

The Crime Scene Investigators (CSI) were busy cordoning off the truck with crime scene tape. They placed small numbered signs by each spent shell and photographed them. As Nutsey was lifted onto a gurney, he regained consciousness for a moment. He tried to say something, but passed out again. Moments later he was on the way to Greenwich Hospital. The sergeant directed me to accompany him back to the City of Rye police station to give a statement.

All area hospitals were notified to contact the City of Rye police department, in the event of a patient seeking treatment for a gunshot wound. Howell called back on my cell phone. He directed me to get back to the office ASAP. He said that he just got off the phone with the DA, and the DA wants to be briefed on the shooting. I told him that I was going to check on Nutsey first. The back stabbing son of a bitch said that I'd better get back to the office as ordered, or he'd bring me up on charges. The guy must have ice water running through his veins. He couldn't give a rats' ass about Nutsey or anyone else for that matter. He's sending a car to pick me up, and drive me to the yard in New Rochelle to pick up the Cadillac.

After I gave a written statement, my weapon was returned. In about a half hour, I was picked up by a squad detective and driven to the yard. Detective Skip Brevis asked if I wanted him to wait while I started the car. I told him that it wouldn't be necessary. As I walked over to my car, the office door flew open. Shorty and an older man briskly walked down the stairs, asking for me to wait a minute. Newcomb huffed gruffly, "Ah Frank, there's someone I'd like you to meet."

The older gentlemen extended his hand. In a raspy voice he said, "I'm Carmine Corso, Gary's father." He looked through me as if I wasn't there. Carmine, in his early sixties, was short and lean. He had an unruly bush of black hair. He stood there studying me.

Then Newcomb, the sinister weasel, in his high pitched voice said, "So Detective Miranda, or whatever your fucking name is, how Nutsey is doing?"

My eyes were riveted on the both of them. "He's gonna be okay. I'm gonna check on him now."

Corso, in a rough tone said, "Tell Nutsey I'm asking for him. Tell him that when I find the guys responsible, I'm gonna chop them up in little pieces. "

Let's say I've been in more comfortable situations and I wanted to get out of there as quickly as I could, but I had to convey a point. "Mr. Corso, I'm sorry about your son and what's happening to Dana, but you can't be the judge, jury, and executioner. Let's let the legal system handle it."

He smirked, pointing a finger in my face. "Oh, but of course detective, you're right. We must let the law handle it."

As I was about to get into the car, Newcomb jumped forward, and in a threatening tone said, "See you around, detective."

They stood there glaring at me, as I drove out of the yard.

It took about a half hour to get to Greenwich Hospital. I walked up to the front desk and asked about Nutsey's status. The receptionist looked through the admittance list and asked if I was a relative. Of course I said yes. She called the nurses station on the third floor and handed me the phone. Again, I was asked if I was related to Louis. I said that I was his cousin. She told me that he'd just come out of surgery and was doing fine, but lost a lot of blood. I asked if I could pop up for a minute to look in on him. They gave me the green light, but said that he was barely awake.

When I walked into room 325, a nurse was hooking Nutsey up to an IV bag. A woman in her fifties sat by his bed with a pair of rosary's in her hand. She introduced herself as Nutsey's sister Debbie Callin. Nutsey's left arm and chest were bandaged down to his waist. I walked over to his bed and gently placed my hand on his arm. "How you doing, Nutsey?"

When he heard my voice, he forced his eyes open and in a muffled voice said, "Okay. I'm okay."

I asked, "Is there anyone else I can call for you?"

He could barely shake his head, but was able to painfully mouth the words, "No Frank. I have no one but my sister, Debbie."

I took his hand, leaning over him. "If you need anything, have your sister call me."

Before closing his eyes, and falling back to sleep, he mumbled, almost in a whisper, "Frank, you're a cop?"

I shook my head yes, and thought to myself, yeah, Nutsey, I'm a cop. I gave Debbie my cell phone number, and then walked out of the room.

CHAPTER SIXTEEN

It was almost 4:30 P.M. when I finally arrived at the court house. As I drove into the parking structure Nulligan called. "Frankie, I heard what happened. You okay?"

"Yeah, Joey, I'm okay, but tired. I just pulled into the parking garage. Hogan wants to see me."

"How's your partner doing?"

"Nutsey, ..." I paused for a second. "Nutsey, he's gonna be okay."

"Yeah, it's too bad, but shit happens."

Trying to process the shooting in my minds eye, I replied, "I feel bad that he got shot. I'm thinking maybe he shouldn't have been on the truck."

"Hey, it wasn't your decision. Hogan signed off on it."
"Yeah, you're right."

"Did you get a look at the scumbags?"

"Yeah, a good look. I shot one of them. The area hospitals are being canvassed to see if the prick shows up."

My phone beeped. "Joe I gotta take the call." It was Howell. "Frank, where are you?"

"I'm in the basement. I'm on my way up."

"We're all in Hogan's office. Get up here right away."

I replied sharply, "I thought you wanted me to report to you first."

He snarled, "Just get up here!"

As soon as Hogan's secretary saw me, she said, "Frank, they're expecting you. Go right in."

Howell, Friedman, and Larry Christopher turned their heads when they heard the door open. District Attorney Hogan stood. "Please have a seat Frank."

I sat down next to Larry. Larry leaned into me, nodding hello and said, "Hey Frank, you look like you've been to hell and back again."

"I'm fine, Cap. Just a little tired."

Hogan's concern was apparent. "Frank, I'm glad that you're okay. You acted properly. I'm sorry that Louis Fuganza was hurt. Chief Howell has been coordinating the investigation with Chief Wilson of the Rye P D. So far no one has shown up seeking medical treatment at any of the area hospitals. The chief, as well as Zack, has been in telephone contact with Dana Corso."

Keying in on what DA Hogan just said, I asked, "What did Dana say?"

Zack interjected, echoing his conversation with Dana. "Carmine confronted her. He is furious that she put a cop on the truck. He told her that he is going to handle it."

Hogan interjected. "Dana told him that he hasn't been handling his own business lately. She said that she came to us for help because Gary didn't want his kind of help."

Zack added, "Right now, Dana's considering selling the business back to her father-in-law."

Howell, not wanting to be outdone, jumped into the conversation. "Frank, as of right now, she's on her own. And you'll be re-assigned where you're needed."

I was taken aback by Howells remark. I looked directly at the DA, stone-faced, then at Howell and finally looked over at Captain Christopher. I shot back, "Chief, it's hard for me to just walk away. There must be something we can do for Dana."

Howell's tone was hostile. He can't help his piss poor nature. "Frank, we're not a private security company. We can't provide security 24/7. But we will exhaust every effort to solve the murders."

I was thinking that we have a moral obligation to help Dana no matter what. What if Dana was Howell's daughter? What would he do? Hang her out to dry?

The fact of the matter is that we can't protect Dana 24 hours a day, 7 days a week. And now that everybody knows that a cop is no longer driving for her, she is a sitting duck. Maybe Gary's father, Carmine, is her only way out of this mess.

Hogan must have sensed the contempt I have for Howell by the look on my face. "Frank, I'm afraid that the chief is right. Mrs. Corso will have to do what she thinks is best for herself and her company. Right now we need to find the shooters and persuade them to talk."

I nodded politely, "Huh, I see."

Hogan gestured to Howell and then directed him to allocate a few more detectives to help the Rye police find the shooters. Christopher gave Howell thumbs up and said, "Not a problem, Chief."

You could see that Hogan was intent on moving the investigations along and wasn't shy on making his point. "Gentlemen, so far there's been no progress on the homicides, and by now, the people involved know that we had a cop on the truck. I'm sure they're the kind of folks that are savvy enough to pull back from things, waiting for the right time to make their move. I've instructed Zack to stay in touch with Dana Corso and the New Rochelle detectives. She's to immediately notify the New Rochelle police if she needs assistance. Frank, for the time being, I think you can use the rest. Take it easy for a few days."

I'm thinking, *Rest? Rest is the furthest thing from my mind. I wanted to get the people who shot Nutsey. They're probably the guys responsible for*

138

the triple murders. As far as the New Rochelle detectives go, I have a score to settle with them.

Zack couldn't help but notice that I was uneasy. "Frank, what's up?"

I had to say what I really felt. "Nutsey's shot, and I'm supposed to rest. What's wrong with this fucking picture? I should be out there working on finding the shooter, not watching the world go by."

Howell yelled out, "That's enough detective!"

Hogan understood how I felt. He gestured with his hand, stopping any further comments from Howell. "Frank, its okay. I know how you feel. I'll make sure that we do everything we can to protect Dana Corso. And by the way, I'm directing Captain Christopher to update you with new information on the whereabouts of the people responsible for shooting Mr. Fuganza."

"Thank you Mr. Hogan."

I looked at Howell who had a scowl on his face.

Finally, we all stood. Hogan shook my hand and said, "Frank, nice work. I knew you wouldn't disappoint me. Now go home and get some rest. And that's an order!"

As we were leaving, Howell, put his hand on my shoulder to get my attention. "I want to see you and Captain Christopher in my office."

Larry, a bit confused about another meeting, shrugged his shoulders, as if to say, what now, but replied, "Okay, Chief."

We walked out of Hogan's office. Zack, Captain Christopher, and I stopped for a moment. Howell walked down the hall ahead of us into his office. Larry and I headed there as well. Jennifer Williams was typing on her computer. She smiled, as we walked in. Her sexy figure could get me in trouble if I didn't know better. "The chief is expecting you. Go right in."

Howell had taken his jacket off and thrown it over a chair in the corner of the room. The first thing the arrogant prick said was, "Larry, before you sit down, pat Frank down to see if he's wearing a wire."

Captain Christopher looked upset by Howells comment. He replied, "I can't do that Chief."

I knew Howell was trying to goad me into doing something I'd regret. Larry would be his witness and I'd be gone. I shook my head and sighed. "Ah come on John, come over and pat me down. I'm not wearing shit."

Howell didn't get the reaction he expected. He was definitely pissed off. He shook his finger in my face and shouted, "I can bring you up on charges. The sawed off shotgun you were carrying is illegal and you can forget about the Corvette. Larry, he keeps the Cadillac, and give him his new assignment. Now get out of my office!"

The fat bastard knew how I felt about him. But instead of losing my temper I remained calm. I was cautious how I spoke to him so there'd be no accusations made. The words seemed to flow out of my mouth. "You're just as nasty as Shawn Daniels and look how he ended up."

"Enough! You undercover guys always end up dirty. If you're not taking money, you're taking drugs! Like I said, get out of my office!"

For the time being, he couldn't touch me. Not after Hogan just gave me his support. I couldn't help myself. I gave Howell a parting shot as Larry and I walked out of his office. "Chief, remember what goes around comes around." I made it a point to slam the outer door as we walked out.

On the elevator ride to the squad room, I stared at the floor, hardly able to believe that guys like Howell actually ran things around here. Larry said something, but I wasn't paying attention. The elevator doors opened. Larry looked over and said, "Frank, are you with me?"

I nodded yes. "Can you believe that jackass?"

As we entered the squad room, I asked, "Larry, what's the new assignment?"

"Come into my office and pull up a chair." We walked the short distance to his office, and I slid a chair in front his desk. He was apologetic. "Frank, I'm so sorry how that nitwit behaved. He was out of line."

"Yeah, I know. But, why is it that guys like him always land on their feet, and other guys end up with the short end of the stick?"

Larry shrugged his shoulders. "Frankie, I just don't know."

"So cap, tell me, what's he having me do now?"

Captain Christopher took a pack of cigarettes from his shirt pocket, tapping the bottom of the pack to firm the tobacco before pulling one out and lighting it. He took a long drag. "You're being assigned to a wiretap. You will be reviewing tape recordings to make sure that the guys are adhering to the minimization requirements. I'll set you up in an empty office. Howell's taking a few detectives from each squad and reassigning them to work on a money laundering case coming out of the Organized Crime Squad. The target is Dante Malatesta, a Genovese soldier. Since you know what these guys are about, the district attorney wants you involved."

"Who will be the ADA supervising the case?"

"Zack."

"That's good. Zack knows his shit. I have another question. Who is assigned from narcotics?"

"Besides you? Nulligan and Serrano. Joe and Angel along with detectives from other squads will cover the meets that are generated from the wire. It's 24/7, but you'll only be working days."

"Interesting," I mumbled. "Funny, Carmine Corso runs a crew in the Genovese family. It'll be interesting to see where this thing goes."

"Frank, like I said, you've got to make sure that the guys sitting the wire adhere to the minimization requirements. We can't record privileged conversations which include conversations between the target and his wife, his lawyer, priest or minister, doctor, psychologist or psychiatrist. If any of these conversations are recorded, it could jeopardize the investigation when and if it goes to trial. The law does state that we're allowed to listen into privileged conversations every minute or so to make sure the parties are not talking about criminal activity. If their conversation becomes criminal, it can be recorded. After each tour of duty, the protocol is that the detective sitting the wire removes the log sheets, the tapes, dates and initials the tapes, assigns them a number, and copy's each tape for your review. The original tape and log sheets are then entered into evidence. Pertinent conversations that are captured will be transcribed by the detectives in the Intelligence Squad, for court purposes. The transcriptions will also be passed onto Zack for his review."

"Cap, it sounds simple enough."

"Look, it's not rocket science, but when you're reviewing the tapes, you'll be comparing the conversations seized with its corresponding log sheets to make sure that everything jives. The log sheet will reflect the detective who recorded the conversation, the date and time of the recording, and a brief synopsis of the conversation captured. Zack has to know immediately if a privileged conversation has been recorded. If one of the detectives missed anything pertinent, bring it directly to Zack's attention."

"Fine, but I have a question."

"Shoot."

"What do I do with the copies of the log sheets and tapes after I'm finished with them?"

"Give them to Zack. He'll store them in his office."

"So when does this all start? And where's the plant located?"

Larry took one last drag of his cigarette and ground it into the ashtray. "The plant will be set up in the locker room. We'll make space next to the bunk beds for a desk and the equipment. The order should be signed tomorrow, and we'll be up and running. Come in on Wednesday morning. You'll have a day of recordings to listen to."

"Okay cap. Is there anything else?"

"That's about it." He said as he fiddled with his desk drawer that seemed to be stuck.

I stood, about to leave, and told him that I was stopping by Jake's for a drink before heading home. I asked him if he wanted to join me. He said that he still had a lot to do and would take a rain check.

There were a few assistant's burning the midnight oil when I left the building. I had a fleeting thought that Denise was home worrying, and that I should go straight home. However, I decided to stop at Jakes for a drink to take the edge off.

By the time I pulled up in front of Jakes it was almost 7:30 P.M. Before walking into the bar, I took off my sweatshirt, leaving it and the gun locked in the car. The night was muggy and hot. It was the beginning of July, and the air conditioned bar felt refreshing. The bar happened to be crowded. I looked around to see if Joe was here. Nulligan was sitting in his usual booth in the dining room, chewing on steak fries and a cheeseburger. Jessica was standing over him in conversation.

"Frankie, slide in. You look like you've been through the mill."

Jessica gave me the once over and said, "You don't look well. You're white as a ghost. What can I get you?"

"Just tired. I'll have a club soda with a twist of lime."

She gently put her hand on my arm and quickly slid it off as she walked back to the bar. Joe was three sheets to the wind. He slurred his words as he said, "Jesus, pal, club soda?" What's wrong? Has Shake- N- Bake taken a pound of your flesh?" Joe took a hefty swig of beer, emptying his glass, and waved to Jessica to bring another beer.

She brought the drinks over, smiled and said jokingly, "Joe, you have to tell him about last night. He's not going to believe it."

Joe looked down into his beer glass, hesitating.

"Joe, so what happened last night? Don't keep me in suspense."

Joe was tipsy as his tongue twisted around his words. "First, I want to hear what Howell had to say."

I gave Joe a rock steady look for a second. The image of Nutsey with a bullet hole in his chest was bouncing around my brain like loose marbles.

"So, what did Howell say?" Joe asked, tilting to one side as he slurred his words.

I could have read him a laundry list of my mind bending meeting with Howell. "Well, for starters, he asked Larry to check me for a wire. Then he had the balls to say that cops like me end up taking money or drugs. Plus the shaky fuck isn't giving me the Corvette back. I gotta keep the Cadillac." As I'm telling Joe, I'm getting more and more upset. "But, Joe, this one takes the cake, the mother fucker considered bringing me up on charges because I carry a sawed-off shotgun. If Larry wasn't there I'd of tore the weasels head off."

Joe almost spun out of the booth, boiling mad, his voice raised, first he mumbled something that I didn't understand, but then with frightening clarity he yelled, "That scumbag should be ashamed of himself!"

Everyone in the dining area turned around glancing over at our booth, but they had enough sense not to say anything. Joe was furious. He waved the waitress over ordering another Blue Point. Joe realized that he was out of control and apologized to the waitress for being loud. He looked at me with fire in his eyes and said, "Bucking the system is like shoveling shit against the tide. You can't win."

"Joe, you're right. But why don't you finish your hamburger? Don't you think you've had enough to drink?"

Joe nodded yes. "You're right Frankie. I've had enough. So what's next for you? You can't continue driving the truck. They all know that you're a cop."

"I've been assigned to an OC wire. I'm reviewing the tapes to make sure that the guys sitting the wire adhere to the minimization requirements. Christopher told me that you and Angel are assigned to one of the surveillance teams."

Joe clumsily reached for his empty beer glass, picked it up, looked at it for a split second, and put it down. Joe was so drunk that he had trouble focusing his eyes on me. However, he was able to mutter, "S-s-so that's why Larry has me an-a- and Angel coming in for a briefing in the morning."

I gulped the glass of club soda down, knowing that I had to get home. "C'mon Joe, tell me what went on last night. I gotta get home."

I don't know how, but Joe managed to tell me that he, Angel, and a few guys from the squad had a drug buy last night. Angel bought a kilo of cocaine from this Dominican guy who lives in Tarrytown. The Dominican gave up that his supplier lives in Flushing, Queens keeps a stash of cocaine in his basement apartment. By the time they finished debriefing him, it was already after midnight and they needed to reach a judge to sign a search warrant for the guy's apartment. Angel called Judge Nicholls, explaining the situation. The Judge said that in order to save time they should stop by his house in Pelham and he'd sign the search warrant. Nicholls said that they could bring him the affidavit in the morning. After leaving the judges house, he and Angel drove to the 109th Precinct in Flushing, requesting a few officers accompany them to execute the warrant. The on duty Sergeant advised Joe and Angel that it is policy that all warrants are executed by Emergency Services.

After reviewing the warrant, Sergeant DiMarzo contacted ESU. Joe and Angel took a seat, anxiously awaiting ESU's arrival for over an hour. Frustrated, they finally said, "Fuck it," and decided to hit the apartment themselves.

They drove down the street to 3795 Union Street. It looked like a three-or-four-family house. As they pulled into the driveway, they noticed that the basement door was to the left of the front steps. They drew their weapons and approached the house. A beam of light shone through the basement door jamb. Joe banged on the door several times, announcing, "Police, open the door," but no one answered. Finally after a minute or so, Angel kicked the door in and they ran into the one room shithole. The next thing Joe saw was this little Hispanic guy, only 5'3'', pencil thin black mustache, in his undershorts. The guy looked as if he was about to crap in his Fruit of the Looms. The little bastard ran across the room to the far wall; the son of a bitch grabbed a bow and arrow off the wall. He quickly turned around, put the arrow in the bow, and shot an arrow, nearly missing Joe by an inch. Joe lost it. The expression on this prick's face was one of terror when he saw Joe coming at him like a run-away train. He grabbed the little fuck by his nuts and throat, picked him up over his head, and threw him against the wall. The guy let out a blood curdling scream that was probably heard down the street in the station house. He bounced of the wall and hit the coffee table a few feet away, smashing it into pieces.

Joe grabbed the guy by the neck and did the tarantella on his head, all the while demanding, "Where's the fucking cocaine?" He said that Angel had to stop him from killing the guy. The mother fucker mumbled something in Spanish, and cried out, "No hablo Englese. No hablo Englese." Joe said that Angel started rattling off in Spanish, asking him where he's hiding the coke. He just laid there shaking his head, "No drugs, no drugs, por favor."

Angel brought in a fire axe he kept in his trunk for special occasions. Joe cuffed the guy, as Angel began chopping the furniture into pieces, while yelling, "Shoot at us with a bow and arrow you dirt bag. I'll find the fucking cocaine."

By this time, Joe has sobered up somewhat and said, "Frankie, when I tell you that Angel chopped up all of the guy's furniture, it's an understatement."

The apartment looked like it had been through Hurricane Andrew. By the time they left, the guy's couch, television, and bedroom set, were in tiny little pieces. But the guy was right. There was no cocaine in his apartment. Angel picked the degenerate up by the cuffs and dragged him out to the car in his underwear, tossing him in the back seat. Joe grabbed the bow and arrow as evidence, and they drove back to the precinct to book him. They dragged him up the precinct steps and threw him in front of the desk sergeant. He was charged with attempted murder of a police officer and resisting arrest. Joe said that he and Angel just got back from Queens. The Queens ADA wanted to see the signed search warrant and the DD 14 documenting the arrest. As Joe was about to continue, Denise called me. She was upset, and sounded worried.

"Hey."

"Frankie, where are you? I've been calling you all day. The shooting is all over the radio and TV."

I didn't have the energy to tell her that I was unable to answer her calls today. "Honey, I'm fine. I stopped at Jake's and hooked up with Joe for a quick drink. I was just leaving."

She sounded very upset. "You didn't think I'd be worried? I'm not important enough to call? You're out drinking with Joe instead of coming home. Frankie, I'm here for you and you're not letting me in." She slammed the phone down.

Joe could hear her on the phone. He looked at me as if to say, you poor fuck.

As I got up to leave, my fucking phone rang again. I recognized the number as Dana Corso's. I let the call go to voice mail. She left a message that she wanted to see me. Joe cleared his throat asking curiously, "Who's it now?"

"Nobody." I turned and walked away.

CHAPTER SEVENTEEN

When I got home from Jake's, the apartment it was dark. I turned on the lights and walked into the bedroom. Denise was asleep, or she was pretending to be asleep. Rather than waking her up and maybe continuing the argument, I decided to grab a pillow and blanket from the closet and sleep on the couch. It was about eleven the next morning when I was awakened by a throbbing headache. To make things worse, I had a stiff neck from sleeping with my head squished between the arm rest and my pillow. I sat up on the couch for a minute, holding my head in my hands, rubbing my temples. The sunlight was so bright that morning I had to squint just to see. Eventually, I got up and drew the curtains in the living room. As I headed for the bathroom to take a few aspirins, I noticed from the corner of my eye, an envelope leaning on a glass vase on the kitchen table.

I stumbled into the kitchen and quickly opened it. It was from Denise. The content of the letter set me on my heels. She said that she needed time to sort things out and think about our life together. She wrote that she would be staying with a girlfriend from work for a while. The letter fell from my hand onto the floor. I was overcome with a deep feeling of isolation.

I couldn't escape from my cell phone. It haunts me 24/7. At that moment, it rang. It was Zack. I was forced to pay attention to what he had to say. Zack was upbeat. "Frank, sorry to bother you on your day off, but there's something I thought you should know."

I must have sounded down. I didn't want to explain that Denise had just walked out on me. "What's going on?"

Zack, breathing hard, said, "The State Special Prosecutor called Hogan's office this morning and said that both Annette Larson and Shawn Daniels decided to plead guilty as charged, rather than go to trial."

"Wow!" I shouted. "There's a God after all."

He continued, "Larson is being disbarred and is sentenced to one year in the State Correctional Facility for Women in Bedford Hills. Daniels got three years in Sing-Sing Prison."

I thought to myself, maybe now, the office can put the whole mess to rest. Barely able to contain my excitement, despite the fact that Denise had left me, I replied, "That's great news, Zack. Thanks for letting me know."

"No problem, Frank." and he hung up.

There was a bottle of aspirins in the medicine cabinet. I took three. Fuck, my phone rang again. I downed three aspirins and rushed back into the living room. It was Dana Corso. "Hey, Dana. How are you?"

She sounded desperate. "Frank, I need to see you right away. Can you stop by my house?"

"Why, what's up?"

"Please. Please. Can you stop by? I need to talk to you."

"Okay, I'll be over in an hour."

"Thank you. Please hurry."

The aspirin and cold shower helped. They seemed to snap me back to where I could at least function. As I dressed to leave, I was absorbed in thought. The idea of losing Denise and my kids was bouncing around my brain. And the worst thing about it was that I had no one to talk to. I wondered how my life was going to end up. It made no sense. But for me nothing makes sense anymore and I realized that nothing stays the same. When I closed the apartment door behind me, the reality of coming home to an empty place hit me like a ton of bricks. But somehow I'd have to handle it. I always do.

Dana was waiting at the front door when I drove up. I was getting out of the car, when I noticed she was barefoot, dressed in a black crew-neck sweater, and skintight white slacks. She held out her hand, anxious for me to hurry in. "Frank thanks for coming. Please come in."

149

She led me through a magnificent marble hallway and into the living room where she gestured with her hand for me to take a seat on a long leather couch. I couldn't help but notice the grand piano, and asked her if she played. With a faint smile she said, "I used to, but not anymore." The room was naturally lit by the sun that streamed through a large glass double door overlooking an opulent slate terrace. She asked if I wanted anything to eat or drink. I shook my head no. The thought of food made my stomach turn. Dana then sat down next to me. She sat so close to me that I could feel her breath as she spoke. Crossing her legs, she made it a point to lean into me, almost resting on my shoulder. If it wasn't that I was in love with Denise, I might have taken advantage of the situation. But that wasn't the case. I felt uncomfortable, and immediately asked, "Huh, what's so important?"

"I thought you should know that my father-in-law is really upset with me. He kept harping that I should have never gone to the District Attorney's Office and never had the DA put a cop on the truck. He said that he can't have cops nosing around his business."

"Is that all?"

"No." Her eyes welled up. She took a deep breath and held it for a moment trying to regain her composure, but couldn't. She cried. "He wants me to sell the business back to him for what we paid for it, and I told him that I didn't want to."

"What are you gonna do?"

"What choice do I have?"

"C'mon, isn't the business worth a lot more now?"

"Yes, but I feel like I have to sell. All the drivers are gone and I'm not able to service my customers. I'm losing money and I have outstanding notes on the garbage trucks."

"Dana, I can't wrap my head around this. Why won't your father-in-law give you what's its worth?"

"I don't know. He just won't. I've put out feelers and no one else is interested."

There was nothing left to say, but that I was sorry. Sorry for the whole mess. Dana took my hand and gently squeezed it. I slid away, but she lunged at me and kissed me on my mouth. I looked intensely into her radiant brown eyes and gently pushed her away. "Dana, you're a beautiful woman, and I'd love to make love to you, but I can't. I'm in love with someone else."

She began to weep again, burying her head in her hands sobbing. I felt horrible, but it would have been so wrong of me to take advantage of her. I told her that it's best that I leave. I said that I'd show myself out. As I stood, I placed my hand softly on her shoulder as if to say that I hoped that things would work out for her. I walked away, leaving her weeping on the couch.

The rest of the day, I lay in bed watching TV, hoping that Denise would call. She never did. It wasn't until 11:00 P.M. that I finally had enough and turned off the TV. I'd be starting a new assignment in the morning and hoped that it would help me take my mind off Denise.

CHAPTER EIGHTEEN

The next morning, I walked into Captain Christopher's office. I was up the night before thinking about Denise, and at that moment could care less about the job. I guess I understood that sharing my life was difficult for her to handle, but her walking out, shattered my world.

After a brief conversation with Larry, he showed me to an empty office in the hallway behind the squad room. It had just been vacated by an assistant district attorney who had been transferred to one of the local branch offices. I walked in and looked around. The room was small, dirty, and in need of painting. It had no windows and poor ventilation, but it was my home for the time being. On top of the desk sat a digital audio recorder, tapes captured from the wire yesterday, and a bunch of legal pads that were neatly stacked. Larry again went over the minimization rules and said that if I had any questions about what conversations were privileged to call Zack. As he was about to walk out of the office, he said in a sincere tone, "Frank, this assignment will give you a much needed break. Take advantage of it."

I nodded, and smiled. "I will Cap. Thank you."

I decided to check out the monitoring room, in the locker room, before reviewing the first tape. After all, I had all day to listen to tapes. I walked back into the squad room, past the Tech Squad, and into the locker room where Detective Andrei Achim was seated at a desk, listening in on a call. So as not to disturb Andrei, I quietly stood behind him. He had just intercepted a call that Dante Malatesta made from his uncle's apartment.

Malatesta, the target of the investigation, apparently felt safe using his uncle's phone. He was confident that law enforcement had no idea that he used his uncle's pre-World War II apartment in a building in South Yonkers, New York. His Uncle Dom and wife Simone live in the fifth floor walkup. Intel did a work up on his uncle. Dominick Malatesta had no criminal record and has recently retired from the laborer's union after working almost 40 years. He's 60, average height and weight, and has brownish, grey hair. He drives a late model black Cadillac, registered to his wife.

Detective Achim, a ten-year veteran of the department, just finished making notes on the log sheet of a conversation he recorded when I walked in.

"Hey Andrei, how's it goin?"

He fumbled with the log sheet for a second and said, "Malatesta was on the phone with a guy from Fort Worth, Texas, Spencer Johnstone. He asked Spencer if Pat got there with the money yet. Frankie, the wire is producing fruit already."

It was a good call. I was thinking, we need to find out who Pat is, how much money is involved, and how is he delivering it. I asked Andrei if he knew who was on surveillance today. He said that Joe is out there already, and Angel will be leaving shortly. They're working until five.

"Do we have a mug shot of Dante Malatesta?"

He replied, "Yeah."

Andrei opened the top drawer and took out a blue file folder. Inside the folder was Malatesta's mug shot. Written on the back was his name, date of birth, social security number, and his last known address. To my surprise the son of a bitch lived in Bronxville. I can't believe that I haven't run into him there. From the stats on the back of the photo, he's forty-five and lives at 125 Bell Road, a private house. He's been married to Ann, nee, Brady for ten years, and has no children. He's menacing looking, with jet black hair, and built like a fire plug.

Just then another call came into the apartment. Detective Achim made note of the time, who called, and who answered the call. He put the call on speaker. It was Spencer Johnstone. Malatesta answered. They spoke quickly, in staccato like bursts.

"Yeah"

"Pat just arrived about ten minutes go. He's a little late because of car trouble outside of Fort Worth. I took a quick count. It looks like five hundred thousand dollars."

"That's the number. Tell Pat to take a day and then I want him back here."

"I'll tell him." Spencer hung up.

Detective Achim made the proper entries on the log sheet and then sat back in his chair grinning. "Frankie, this may be a short lived investigation."

I replied with some skepticism, "Yeah, we'll see," as I gave him thumbs up, and walked out of the plant and into my office.

I had a question and gave Captain Christopher a call. "Hey, Cap."

"Yeah, Frank?"

"Is Intel compiling the data on the case, or do you have another squad doing it?"

"No, Intel is handling it."

"Sound's good, Cap. Thanks."

I was about to put headphones on when Angel walked in. "Hey Angel, what's up?"

"Just stopped in to say hello. I'm about to hit the street. Anything new on the shooters? How is Nutsey doing?"

"Nothing new yet on the shooters. I guess Nutsey is doing okay."

"How do you like your new assignment?"

"Angel, it's fucking boring. I hope things pick up."

He winked and said, "Hang in there," as he left.

I was going to put the headphones on, but decided to call my brother instead. I punched in his cell phone number and he answered on the first ring. "Hey, Richie."

"Brother, what's up?"

"Just checking in. How ya doin?"

"I'm okay. Working on an accounting ledger. Trying to find out how this prick cooked the books. How 'bout you?"

I thought it best to tell him that Denise had walked out on me. I explained that she apparently heard about the shooting, and I foolishly didn't take the time out to call, and tell her that I was okay. Richie didn't say much. He didn't have to.

As we were about to hang up, he mumbled under his breath, "I'm sorry, Frankie."

"Me too."

I put on the headphones. It was only noon, and I had a number of tapes to listen to before I could call it a day. After listening to the first tape, I was able to piece together that a guy by the name of Patrick Johns was transporting money for Malatesta. I called Intel and asked them to do a work up on Johns. They were already doing a background on Johnstone.

After four more boring hours of listening to tapes, I decided to call it a day. Before leaving the office, I called Joe and asked him if he and Angel wanted to meet me at Jakes after they got relieved. Joe said that he'd be there, but he wasn't sure about Angel. Before hanging up, I told him that I plan to stop by the hospital to see Nutsey. I spoke to the nurse's station earlier and one of the nurses said that he was doing fine.

CHAPTER NINETEEN

Nutsey had been moved to a shared room. He was sitting in a recliner by his bed, dressed in a hospital gown and bed slippers. As soon as he saw me, his eyes lit up. I smiled and handed him a box of chocolates that I'd bought at the hospitals gift shop. He took the gift box, and placed it on the portable serving table by the bed. There was pain in his eyes as he looked up at me. "Thanks, Frank."

I reached down and gave him a friendly pat on his shoulder. "How are you holding up?"

He replied in a muffled voice, "I'm feeling better. And there's no infection. I should be out of here in a few days."

I drew the other patient's curtain for privacy. Nutsey asked me to pour him a glass of water. He cleared his throat, and said with his Popeye smile, "Damn, I shoulda figured something was up when you said that you'd never driven a garbage truck."

I chuckled and said, "I said what I had to say." By the way, I've got some bad news. Dana plans to sell the business. If she doesn't, the consequences could be devastating for her. I'm sure you understand."

He replied, keying in on what I just said, "I know. She could be in serious trouble. Carmine paid me a visit this morning. He told me that Dana was selling the business to him. He said that I have a job waiting for me when I'm ready to come back to work. The guy doesn't seem right to me. I guess it's because of Gary's murder. He's been acting weird for the last six months. Before he left, he asked me if I knew that you were a cop. I told him no. I had no idea. He muttered, "Santorsola, huh", as he left.

"Well, um, Nutsey, maybe you can find a job with another company?"

Nutsey's head dropped down and he frowned. "Frank, it won't be easy finding another job."

I reached for Nutsey's hand and told him I had to leave. "You never know until you try." He smiled. "Frank thanks for stopping by." As I was walking out, he took a parting shot. "Frank, I shoulda known you were a cop."

Joe was already there when I walked into Jake's. As soon as Jessica saw me she asked, from behind the bar, "Frankie, what will ya have?"

I hollered, "Dewar's with ice."

As slid into the booth opposite him, I asked Joe if Angel was stopping by. He shook his head no. Angel had to go to Home Depot to pick up some nails for a project he was working on. Joe asked curiously, "What's up? If you wanted to meet, it must be important."

"Well," I said, "Nothing happening with finding the shooters. I'd like to start looking for them myself, but I can't. I'm locked in the office listening to tapes." Bobby McCarthy placed my drink down, and I quickly downed it.

Joe nodded his head as if to say wow, something is gnawing at you and said, "There are a lot of cops looking for these mutts. Hang tight, they'll find them."

Jessica made it a point to walk over and say hello. She obliviously sensed that there was something going on and asked, "Frankie, how've you been?"

I looked up at her, thinking that this was a good a time to tell them that Denise and I weren't an item anymore. I sank in the booth responding despondently, "Denise and I split up."

Jessica's looked stunned. "Oh, Frankie, I'm so sorry to hear that. Is there anything we can do?"

I looked down into my glass, probably looking as if I'd lost my best friend, shaking my head no.

Jessica's voice cracked before walking back to the bar. "Frankie, if Joe and I can do anything please let us know."

"Sure, Jessica. Thanks."

By now, Joe must have had three pints of Blue Point and was feeling no pain. He developed his habit of over indulging his early years. Growing up, he spent many summers in Dublin, Ireland, living with his maternal aunt Khaki Rowland. As a young man he was no stranger to Temple Bar, a bustling mecca for young and old alike. Folk music and booze abound in the Irish pubs.

Just about able to get the words out, Joe said, "I'm sorry to hear about you and Denise.

I nodded yes.

"By the way, you stopped to see Nutsey, how's he doing?"

"Nutsey's okay. He's being released from the hospital in a few days."

At that moment I had a thought to call Dana Corso. I punched in her number on my cell phone. After several rings, she answered, sounding depressed. "Hello."

"Hey Dana, this is Frank."

"Hi Frank."

"Dana, I've got a favor to ask."

"Oh, what is it?"

"Nutsey will be released from the hospital in a day or so. Carmine offered him his job back. I'd rather he not work for him. Can you find him something to do?"

She didn't respond for a second. Then the tone of her voice rose. "It's funny you asked. I'm looking for a full time handyman and was just about to place an ad in the local paper."

Feeling good that I did Nutsey a favor, I replied, "Well, now, you don't have to place the ad."

"Ah, I guess I don't. I'll call Nutsey in the morning and discuss it with him."

I settled back in the booth and asked, "Joe how'd the surveillance go today?"

"Frankie, we're beginning to get a handle on Malatesta's daily activities. He usually leaves his house at 11:30 A.M. He stops at Starbucks in Depot Plaza in Tuckahoe for coffee, and drives to his uncle's apartment on Van Cortland Park Avenue in Yonkers. His Uncle Dom leaves the apartment everyday about 12:40 P.M. Dante usually stays until 3:00 P.M. After leaving his uncles apartment today, we followed him to Carmine's yard in Pelham."

I sat up with open ears. "No shit!"

"He drove his Benz into the yard at 3:30 P.M. It looked like Corso was impatient, pacing up and down in the yard waiting for him. They appeared to be having a heated discussion, visibly frustrated, waving their arms in an animated discussion. Angel photographed the whole thing. About 3:50 P.M., Dante jumped back into his car, and we took him home. He stayed there until we were relieved by Harold and Danny."

"Well, well, well. Now we know who Dante answers to."

"Looks that way, Frankie boy."

Things were falling into place quickly. Malatesta appears to be in Carmine's crew, and is probably up to his eyeballs in laundering money from their illegal activities. I had a feeling that things were going to break wide open.

CHAPTER TWENTY

It was July 1st, and it was hot as hell. Joe walked into my office at 9:30 A.M., still hung over from the night before. He and Angel were working the 4:00 P.M. to 12 A.M. shift. I guess he couldn't sleep from his hangover, and rather than sit around his apartment, he came to in to work on his surveillance reports. He walked into my office to let me know that he was in. No sooner than he walked in, there was a loud knock on my office door. It was Captain Christopher. He was surprised to see Joe standing there. "Hey Joe, you're in a little early."

Joe nodded yes and said, "Yes, Cap. I couldn't sleep."

"Yeah Joe, been there, done that."

Larry seemed to be in a rush. He handed me two reports from the Intelligence Squad, and walked out.

Joe, rubbing his temples garbled, "Cheech, you got any aspirins?"

"Not here. I got a bottle in my locker."

As Joe turned to leave, he said "I have a bottle my locker too. Thanks."

As I was about to read the reports, my mind drifted to thoughts of Denise, and what she might be thinking at this very moment. I wondered if she might be thinking about me, and how I was handling her leaving. I was hoping that she'd call. I miss hearing her voice. My eyes drifted down to the Intelligence reports, lying in front of me. The top folder had the name of Patrick Johns written on it. The sight of the reports snapped me out of my depression, and I began to thumb through one of the folders.

Johns' was born in 1939. His mug shot was stapled to the back of the folder. At 6'1", blond hair and blue eyes, he weighs a hefty 230lbs. He lives on the second floor of a two family house at 4601 Murdock Avenue in the North Bronx. His rap sheet reads like a "Who's Who" in organized crime. He's been arrested and convicted for drug smuggling, extortion, labor racketeering, assault with intent to cause bodily injury, loansharking, illegal gambling, burglary, and witness tampering. He has been implicated in several murders, but there was never enough evidence to charge him. Johns has spent a total of thirty of his sixty-five years in either state or federal prison. In the 1970's and 80's, the F.B.I. and the NYPD linked Johns to an Irish American gang, *The Westies*. They operated out of Hell's Kitchen on Manhattan's West Side. The gang had ties with the Gambino Crime Family, at the time run by Paul Castellano. It's alleged that *The Westies* worked for the Gambino's as contract killers. The report stated that in the early 1990's, high ranking members of the gang were charged with murder and other heinous crimes. Rather than face lengthy prison sentences, they cooperated with the government, testified against other members of the gang, effectively leading to the gang's demise. For a number of years, Patrick Johns has successfully stayed below the radar of law enforcement, slipping into obscurity, until now. The evidence seized from our wire shows that Patrick Johns is carrying money to Texas for Dante Malatesta, a Genovese soldier who reports directly to Carmine Corso. Carmine is a long time Capo in the family. I couldn't help but think of Carmine's son's murder and how I wouldn't want to be the people responsible for it.

I then picked up the file on Spencer Johnstone. He was born in Austin, Texas on December 2, 1969. He has no criminal history, and lives with his wife Maureen, nee Sullivan, in the suburbs of Fort Worth. Since 1999, Johnstone has owned and operated Dye-Tech Systems, a company that creates accounting software for corporate and small businesses. Before that, he worked as a computer programmer for PD&P Corporation, a supplier of regional energy based out of Oregon. Spencer and his wife have two boys, Christian 15, and Matthew 10.

Just as I put the folder down, Captain Christopher rushed into my office. "Frank, we just intercepted a call between Malatesta and Johnstone. Johnstone has developed a software program for computerized gambling. He's trying to sell Malatesta on the idea to computerize all his gambling spots, and wants to pitch the idea to Malatesta and his boss."

"Cap, damn that's good news."

He replied with increasing excitement, "Frankie, the way Johnstone explained it, all the bets collected, whether sports or number bets, are manually entered into Johnstone's program by the sheet writer. After all the bets are in, he forwards them to a compatible computer in an undisclosed location. The computer keeps track of the daily winning numbers, winning sporting events, odds on each event, bettors' names, the runner who took the bet, monies wagered, commissions earned, and the monies won and lost. If a wire room is raided by police, the computer has a feature allowing the records to be sent quickly to the main computer housed in remote location in Mexico City, leaving the cops without evidence to prosecute anyone."

"No shit!" I asked Larry what Malatesta thought of the idea.

Larry said that Malatesta liked the idea, and said that's it about time that they entered into the twenty first century. He asked the cost of outfitting each room. Johnstone said his fee is $25,000 per wire room, and $500 a month to service each room in case anything goes wrong with the system.

"Wow," I said as I sat back in my chair, thinking about what Larry had just said. My next question was obvious, "Did Malatesta mention who he had to run the idea by?"

Larry shook his head no, but said, "I think we have a good idea who it is."

"Yes", I nodded grinning. "And his first name is Carmine. Isn't it funny that what goes around comes around?"

Larry winked as he walked out and said, "It sure is."

I put the headphones back on to review another tape, but I couldn't focus on listening to another tape. All I could think of was Denise. It's been several days now, and I haven't heard from her. At this moment, hope replaced self pity and I decided to give her a call. I began dialing her number, but something stopped me. I guess I was afraid of what she might say. I placed the desk phone down into its base. I sat there staring at the phone.

At this juncture into our investigation, there were three surveillance teams sitting on Malatesta's uncles building, one of which was our technical unit. Eavesdropping warrants had been signed, and the technical team was looking for an opportunity to enter Dom's apartment and bug it. The tech guys were outfitted with Cablevision uniforms and ready to break in as soon as the apartment was empty.

I managed to get through the rest of the day without any interruptions. It was almost 5:30 P.M., when I finished the last tape. I made my way down to the basement garage, not wanting to run into anyone. I wasn't in the mood to talk. I got into the Cadillac and sped out of the garage, heading for my apartment.

The apartment felt like a mausoleum. I immediately flicked on the lights and turned on the sound system to listen to some music. After I settled in, I thought that I'd go out and grab a slice of pizza, but on second thought, I didn't have the energy. Instead I took a frozen dinner from the freezer and nuked it in the microwave. I sat in the kitchen, down in the dumps, staring into the container of baked macaroni, trying to force it down my throat, but I just couldn't eat it. I think I only took a forkful of the shit. The rest went into the garbage. I just wanted to go to sleep and forget about everything.

I'd just had fallen asleep, when I got a call. I fumbled round in the dark for the phone on the night stand, and finally got a hold of it.

Joe could hardly talk because of his excitement. "Cheech, its Joe! You're not going to believe it!"

I replied, "What, what time is it?" I'm half asleep."

"It's just after midnight!" He shouted.

"Fuck Joe, you woke me up. What's so fuckin important?"

Joe sounded like he just won the lottery. "Frankie, John Howell has been arrested for giving head to an underage boy in the back seat of his police car."

My eyes shot open. I sat up straight up as if I'd slept soundly for eight hours. "You gotta be kidding me! Where was this? When? Who locked him up?"

Joe went on like he was reading from a Hollywood script. "He was arrested a couple of hours ago by the Greenburg cops behind St. Bartholomew's Catholic Church! It's true. I just got a call from Larry. Howell's been suspended pending the investigation. Larry has been appointed acting chief until this mess gets resolved. But one thing's for sure, that lunatic is gone."

The memories of what he and Daniels had put me through washed through my mind like a buzz saw cutting through an oak tree. Joe started laughing. "The bastard looked like some kind of sexual offender anyway. I just didn't know what kind."

I jumped out of bed as we continued to talk, pacing back and forth with nervous energy. I chuckled to myself, thinking that I wouldn't have to deal with that moron anymore. That back stabbing son of a bitch literally stepped on his own dick. I went back to bed laughing to myself. Howell kept a secret that was finally exposed. God only knows how long and how many victims there are. Everything that was going on seemed to swirl around in my brain, and I couldn't turn it off. It must have been 6:00 A.M. when I finally fell back to sleep. Believe it or not, with the little rest I had, it was one of my best night sleeps in years.

The next morning I walked into the squad room and noticed Larry in his office, stuffing a large cardboard box with his personal items. I stuck my head in and said with a grin, "Congratulations, Chief."

He smiled and said, "I hope I can live up to Hogan's expectations. He's got me handling the chief's job and running the narcotics squad until a permanent captain can replace me. Frank, have you thought about taking the sergeants test?"

I shrugged my shoulders and winced. "No. I sort of like doing what I'm doing."

He looked over at me and said, "You should think about it. You'd make a good supervisor."

I bent down to help pick up a box of Sharpies he'd dropped and handed it to him. "Thanks Cap. I mean Chief."

"Frank, by the way, last night, we got the listening devices installed in the uncle's apartment. The bugs are up and running. Let's hope they're productive. "

"That's great Cap" … pausing, again realizing that he's now the acting chief, I continued, "I mean, Chief."

Larry laughed and said, "I guess it's time to go upstairs." One of the detectives took the box of office supplies out of Larry's hands to carry it out. "Chief, I got it." I followed them to the elevator, and took a swipe at Howell as they stepped into the elevator. "As I always say, It ain't easy, being easy." Howell thought he was above the law, but his lifestyle caught up to him."

The money laundering investigation was in its infancy and we have already obtained a court order to bug the uncle's apartment. Listening devices were placed in the electrical sockets in each room. A device was installed inside the shade of the pole lamp, next to the couch by an end table where the house phone sits. The entry team took less than an hour to install the bugs that will be monitored 24/7 by another group of detectives.

The devices were just installed when Andrei phoned me. He told me that Malatesta was overheard on the living room bug talking to his uncle about his money laundering operation. It looks like his uncle is more involved than we thought. I guess the old saying that blood is thicker than water is true.

Achim tells me that Malatesta was overheard telling his uncle how Patrick Johns drives to Fort Worth every two weeks, delivering between five hundred thousand and eight hundred thousand dollars of the family's drug and gambling money to be laundered. Johns earns two thousand dollars, plus expenses for each trip. The money is dropped off at Johnstone's house where it's then deposited into a Mexican bank where dollars are exchanged for pesos. The Bank officials are in collusion with the group, and are paid handsomely for their cooperation and assistance.

Johns spends only one night in Fort Worth and then heads back to New York. The way it works, Spencer passes the money through a currency exchange company, Casa Del Cambio, in Dallas. They wire the money to Banco National in Mexico City, to be exchanged for pesos. The pesos are wired into an American shell company of Spencer's in Fort Worth. The laundered money is then wired out of Texas to a phony mortgage company in New York City that one of Malatesta's cronies run. Spencer's end is five thousand dollars for each transfer. It's truly a lesson in how the wise guys insulate themselves and clean their dirty money. I thanked Andrei for the heads up and asked him the question that we all want an answer to. "Has Carmine been discussed?"

"No. But, Dante told his uncle that his skipper is losing it. He said that his boss's girlfriend is giving him a problem, big time. After three years together, he suspects she has another man in her life. He's having her followed. He's obsessed with this girl. All he talks about is her and who she's seeing. He's neglecting the business."

"Andrei, you know who he's talking about. We got Dante meeting with Carmine. Corso has got to be his skipper."

"Looks that way Cheech. We'll see."

I put the headphones back on and began to review the next tape. Malatesta was to talking to a guy named Paulie Gallione. Again, this conversation was a real insight into how these guys think and operate. Malatesta tells Gallione that he plays poker every Sunday night in the Bronx, in a social club on Westchester Avenue. Malatesta is emotionally absorbed as he tells Gallione about Primo, who is winning big at this poker game. He says that every time Primo wins a big pot, he laughs like he just got away with fucking his best friend's wife. Now as I'm listening to Malatesta bellow to Gallione, I'm thinking that Malatesta is nobody to fuck with. Malatesta rambled on about Primo, saying he excused himself from the table to find out who this guy was. He asked someone at the bar if Primo was a connected guy. He was told that the guy's a nobody. He was brought to the game by Dean Pasienzo. Unfortunately, Primo couldn't keep his big mouth shut. I'm guessing by the conversation; it was just a matter of time before Dante gave him an old fashion ass kicking. I was right. Malatesta tells Gallione that he sits back down as Primo continues to win pot after pot, rubbing everybody's face in it. Finally, Malatesta said that he had enough of this jackass's shit. He jumps out of his seat, grabs a bottle of scotch from the bar, and smashes the bottle over the poor fucker's head, knocking him out cold. He laughs, telling Gallione that while Primo's passed out on the floor, he reaches into the guy's pocket, takes his money, spits on him, and walks out of the club.

As I was putting the tape away, I got a surprise visit from John Hogan. He knocked on the door and walked in. I gestured for him to pull up a chair and sit down. "Hey Mr. Hogan what a surprise, please have a seat. What can I do for you?"

The DA was truly a clotheshorse. Dressed to the nines, he grabbed a seat and said, "Frank, I just wanted to stop by and see how you were doing. I want you and every detective in the squad to know that I don't sit there on the fifth floor in my ivory tower taking you for granted. You guys do a tremendous job, and I want you to know that I appreciate it."

I was taken aback. I didn't know what to say. Stammering for a split second I replied, "Thank you Mr. Hogan. That's very refreshing to hear."

He looked around the office for a moment before he left and said, "Frank you should think about taking the sergeants exam, huh. We need leaders."

Where have I heard that before? He must have been taking to Larry Christopher.

CHAPTER TWENTY ONE

The following day, Chief Christopher phoned me, and asked to meet him in Hogan's office. While I waited to be buzzed in, I made small talk with Corrine and the uniformed police officer. I didn't have to wait long. "Frank, the DA will see you now."

Hogan was seated with his sleeves rolled up, his Burberry tie loosened at the neck. Acting Chief Christopher was sitting in front of his desk. Hogan gestured with his hand for me to take a seat. "Frank, take a seat and make yourself comfortable. You're probably wondering why the chief asked you to my office, so I'll get right to the point. We may have gotten a break on the garbage murders."

Now that got my attention.

"Why don't you tell him, chief?"

Larry paused for a moment before he spoke. "Frankie, it looks like these homicides might be solved after all. As you know, Carmine Corso is in the process of buying the carting company from his daughter-in-law. She'll be officially out of the business soon. For the past few days, New Rochelle Detectives Straub and Barry have had C& C Carting under surveillance. The other night, they observed Shorty Newcomb leaving the office, carrying a large plastic garbage bag. He was followed to the Bronx River Parkway where he headed south into the Bronx, exiting at Allerton Avenue. They followed him to the White Castle burger joint on Boston Road, across the street from Gino's Restaurant. According to Straub, Newcomb pulled around the back of White Castle and parked. He opened his trunk, took out the plastic garbage bag, and tossed it into the dumpster behind the restaurant. The detectives speculated that Newcomb, being paranoid, had hidden the bag somewhere safe, before dumping it. After Newcomb drove away, the detectives waited a short while before retrieving the bag. Detective Barry opened it and found a pair of bloodstained denim jeans, and a bloody sweatshirt. The clothes are being tested at Westchester County lab for DNA, as we speak. We should know something soon."

I sat there wrestling with the thought that maybe Newcomb is a killer. I piped up, "Maybe we got our killer. Kudos to the PD." But, I knew that I still have a score to settle with those cowboys. After all, it's not every day that somebody sticks a gun to your head.

Hogan's phone rang. He excused himself and answered the call. Placing his hand over the mouth piece, he said in a quiet steady voice, "Sorry gentlemen, I have to take this call. We'll talk again."

Larry and I stood. As we walked out, Larry said, "I'll keep you posted boss."

I winked at Corrine, as I returned to my office. It wasn't long before Detective Achim called me and said that he'd just intercepted an interesting call. Johnstone had telephoned Malatesta and told him that the last shipment of money was short by two thousand dollars. Johnstone wanted to know if the count in New York was accurate. Malatesta was emphatic about the count being accurate. He said that the only way that it could be off is if the money counter malfunctioned, and that was highly unlikely. Dante said that he'd have the money counter checked. He told Johnstone that if Johns took the money, he'd cut his balls off, and stuff them down his throat.

The rest of the day was uneventful, although at times I had a few laughs listening to some of the conversations between Malatesta and his gumbas. On one of the tapes, Malatesta was talking to one of his wire room operators. Apparently Dante owns a pig farm upstate, in Monticello, New York. Malatesta tells the guy that his brother's daughter, who's only twenty-five, had recently lost her husband to brain cancer. He said that he was trying to fix up her up with a numbers runner who had just started working for him. Malatesta laughed and said he used a pretext of repairing a fence to get the kid up there. He tells the kid to drive up on Sunday morning to help repair a fence. Still laughing, he said that the kid can't say no. He goes on to tell the wire-room operator that he gave the kid the address, phone number, and not to tell anyone about the farm because, as he put it, every other person works for the F.B.I. Malatesta said that while he's working on the fence, the kid arrives. By the way, he never gives up the kid's name. But he does say that he's about the same age as his niece, single, of Italian decent, making good money from running numbers, and selling the loot from his burglaries. He said that because this kid can think on his feet, he plans to groom him for bigger and better things in the life. Malatesta begins to laugh. He said that he and the kid had been re-nailing the railings for about an hour when his niece Maria opens the front door of the house, and yells out, "Uncle Dante, the macaroni's ready." He's telling the wire-room operator that his niece must weigh three hundred pounds, is five feet tall by five feet wide, and is so fat that the moles on her face look like chocolate chips. When the kid got a glimpse of the niece, he froze in his tracks and his mouth hung open. Malatesta and the wire-room operator are laughing hysterically. Malatesta tells the kid that the real reason he had him come up, is to meet his niece. She needs a husband. He said that the kids face begins to contort as if he's afraid he'll be forced to marry the girl. Then he said the kid started to stutter. "Wa…. wa…with… all….d...d...d... due respect. I got a girlfriend. We're la...la...like living together." I wasn't able to decipher the rest of what the kid said. Malatesta said that he told the kid that if he marries his niece, he'll have a future in the family. Malatesta went on to say that when they walked into the house, the kid was so nervous that he didn't look at his niece once. The wire-room guy asked Malatesta if the kid stayed for dinner. Malatesta said that the kid complained of a stomachache, doubled over, and held his stomach in pain. He said that the kid took another look at his niece, and ran out of the house like Satan himself was chasing him.

CHAPTER TWENTY TWO

Nulligan called me early the next morning and told me to hurry into the office. The homicide case was breaking wide open. Friedman wanted to see me right away. I begged Joe to tell me what was going on, but he wouldn't. I couldn't help but ask, "Did we get a DNA match on Newcomb's clothes? C'mon Joe, tell me."

He laughed. "Huh, look Frankie; Zack wants to tell you himself. Just get in here. We'll talk later. I don't want to miss Malatesta this morning." His phone clicked off.

On the way into the office, I wanted to call Denise, but I guess it's a male thing, my pride got in the way. I rolled into the underground parking garage about 8:30 A.M., and hurried to Zack's office. Excited to the point of frustration, I huffed, "So what's so important that Joe couldn't tell me over the phone?"

Zack smirked and said, "You need to sit and brace yourself." We got a DNA match on Newcomb's clothes. It's Gary Corso's blood! Straub and Barry are picking Newcomb up as we speak. They'll be here any minute."

In a booming voice I yelled, "Shit! Is he going to be charged?"

Zack calmly said, "We're going to try to sweat a confession out of him first. We'll have to see."

Just then, Zack's phone rang. He picked it up, and with his other hand, he gave me a thumbs up and said, "Its Detective Barry. They're pulling into the underground parking garage. They want to know where to take him." Zack told them to take him to the fourth floor and wait by the receptionist. He'd be right out.

I so was excited, I began fidgeting with a pen, clicking it nonstop, until Zack couldn't stand it any longer, and asked me to stop. Zack suggested that I monitor Newcomb's interview from the next room that was wired for sound and equipped with a two-way mirror. Zack left his office for the reception station and I headed for the room to listen to what Newcomb had to say.

Newcomb looked glum when he was escorted in handcuffs into the drab interrogation room. Detective Straub removed the cuffs and seated Newcomb across the table from Zack. Straub placed shackles on Newcomb's ankles. A digital audio recorder sat in the middle of the table next to a phone. The room was also outfitted with audio and video equipment controlled from the technical services room down the hall. At the same time that all this is going on, an affidavit to search Newcomb's apartment and car was being prepared. The first thing the arrogant little prick said was, "You guys got nuttin on me. What's this all about?"

Zack let Newcomb know who was controlling the interview. "First of all, Mr. Newcomb, let me introduce myself. I am Assistant District Attorney Zack Friedman. My office, in conjunction with the New Rochelle police department, is investigating the murders of Leonard Capolla, Gary Corso and Clare Iverson."

Newcomb blurted out in his rough voice, "What do I know? I got nuttin' to do with it!"

Detective Straub, who was seated next to Newcomb, slammed his hand on the table. "We have your clothes that you dumped at White Castle! Gary's blood and DNA is all over them. Do you want to tell us how it got there?"

Newcomb's face muscles began to twitch. As cold as ice, he replied, "I want to speak to my attorney."

At that instant, Zack shouted, "No more questions!" and handed him the phone.

In the interim, a no-knock search warrant had been signed. Two teams of detectives were on their way to search Newcomb's apartment, at 654 White Plains Road, Bronx, NY. According to the detectives, Newcomb's girlfriend, Jean Miller, answered the door of apartment 6J, saving them the trouble of knocking it down. She's a bit overweight and very hard to look at. Still in her robe, she copped an attitude, demanding to know what this travesty of justice was all about. She wouldn't stop her tirade, became unruly and was dragged into the kitchen, where she was forced to sit at the kitchen table. The detective who was assigned to keep an eye on her said that she drove him crazy. He told Friedman that Ms. Miller was mouthing profanities all during their search. Unfortunately after a few hours of searching the one-bedroom apartment, they found no additional evidence linking Shorty to the murders. On their way out, a copy of the search warrant was left on the kitchen table for their attorney's review. Ms. Miller was so irate as they walked out, she hurled a trash basket at them, nearly hitting one of the detectives.

About 1:30 P.M., Newcomb's Attorney, Aidan Rose, a young, beautiful, fair-haired, defense attorney, showed up at the Court House. She was escorted into the interrogation room by Friedman. Ms. Rose immediately asked to speak to her client in private. Zack, Detectives Barry and Straub, pushed away from the table, stood, and walked out of the room. This was my chance to have a friendly chat with Detective Straub. I met them in the hallway. When they saw me they did a double take. I huffed, "Hey fellows, remember me?"

I lunged at Straub, shoving him against the wall, taking hold of his shirt collar, and twisting so he couldn't breathe. Friedman and Barry stood there stunned. "The next time you'd better think twice before you put a gun against someone's head!" You're fucking public servants! Your badge doesn't give you a license to brutalize people. Get it?"

Detective Straub didn't say a word as I held him up against the wall. Friedman got between us and managed to pull me off of him. Breathing hard, Straub looked at me with a twenty mission stare. Then he slowly straightened his tie, and followed Zack and Detective Barry back into the interrogation room. I took a deep breath and re-entered the adjacent room to watch the rest of Newcomb's sideshow.

When they were seated, Newcomb's lawyer said that her client was ready to talk. Zack turned the digital audio recorder on, asking Detective Barry to advise Newcomb of his constitutional right to remain silent. Newcomb's attorney stopped Detective Barry and said that her client is waiving his rights. We were all ears. Newcomb began by saying that he dumped his bloody clothes in the dumpster so that he wouldn't be in the situation that he's in now. He did admit that the blood on his clothes belongs to Gary, but it got there when he came to Gary's aid after Gary was shot the first time. He said that he had nothing to do with Gary's murder or anyone else's.

Zack, looking like the wind had just been sucked out of him, asked to speak with the detectives in the hallway. They slowly walked out of the room looking dejected. I joined them in the hallway. Detective Straub put his up his hand as if to say, enough already. Zack leaned against the wall, dropped his head and said glumly, "We have to cut him loose. We can't prove that Gary's blood got on Newcomb's jeans at the time of his death."

Needless to say, we were all devastated. We thought that we had Shorty by the shorthairs. We thought we'd finally found Gary's killer.

Newcomb smirked as Detective Barry unshackled him, and said coldly, "I told ya, you got nuttin on me. Let's get out of here Aidan." Straub and Barry reluctantly escorted them to the main elevator, and they left the building.

CHAPTER TWENTY THREE

The squad was bummed out because Newcomb walked and we were no closer to solving the killings. I went back to reviewing the tapes. I was getting a closer look into Malatesta's personality and learning what made the evil son of a bitch tick. When it came to running his illegal businesses, he was ruthless. On one of the tapes, I heard Malatesta tell a loan shark victim, Charles Mangione, that if he didn't come up with his weekly vig, he'd drink his blood. As I listened, Mangione begged for more time.

Chief Christopher walked into my office. I was so focused on the conversation; I didn't hear him walk in. Larry tapped me on the shoulder to get my attention and, with a look of excitement, told me that a few hours ago a call was intercepted from Spencer Johnstone asking if Malatesta had considered his proposal for computerizing the wire rooms. According to the chief, Malatesta told Spencer that he was very interested in his proposal. A few of his associates wanted to see a demonstration. Malatesta was adamant that the person responsible for protecting the Mexico City end of the operation be there. Dante specifically wanted to understand how their records, once downloaded to Mexico City could be retrieved. Spencer said that if the bets have to be downloaded to Mexico City because of a police raid, the bets can be sent back to the States, the same way they came, via computer. Spencer told Malatesta that Hugo Zapata-Feliz, a captain in the Mexican Federal Police will be paid to run interference with the Mexican police. He said that their operation will run with impunity. Spencer went on to say that he has stayed at the Mirage Hotel in Las Vegas many times and it will be a good place to set up the demonstration. He said that he would have Zapata-Feliz attend the meeting for any questions that they may have. Malatesta told Spencer that he'd let him know when to set up the meeting. The chief said that he wanted me to fly to Vegas. "Frankie, we want you to observe the meeting. I've contacted the Metropolitan Police in Vegas and detectives from their Intelligence Division will assist us in identifying the wise guys who show up for the demonstration."

I've got to be careful. Carmine Corso knows me and if he shows up, and sees me, the investigation is blown. It was a done deal. I was going to Vegas. For the next several days I continued to monitor tapes, waiting for

Malatesta to contact Spencer. On Friday, Malatesta called Spencer's home, telling him that he and his friends were flying to Las Vegas on the weekend, and to be ready on Sunday night to demonstrate his program. He insisted that Hugo Zapata-Feliz be there or there would be no meeting. I wanted desperately to let Denise know that I was going out of town, but I still couldn't bring myself to call her.

The Vegas police began checking the passenger manifests for all flights into Las Vegas on that weekend looking for Malatesta's name. Three teams of detectives were assigned to follow the targets from the airport to the Mirage Hotel and shadow them during their stay in Vegas. My office arranged a flight for me on American Airlines arriving at McCarran International Airport at 3:00 P.M. on Saturday. I'd be met at the airport by a detective from the Intelligence Division and driven to their headquarters. I packed a carry-on, containing a change of clothes and some personal hygiene items, and my 9mm. At 10:00 A.M. on Saturday, I was picked up at my apartment by a squad detective and driven to Kennedy Airport.

As luck would have it, Dante Malatesta enters the plane and sits four rows in front of me. Even though I needed to use the restroom, I ducked down in my seat for the five-hour flight to Vegas. Dante doesn't know who I am and I want to keep it that way.

Detective Tyra Williams was assigned to meet me at the gate. To protect my identity, she held up a sign with her first name written on it. Guys like Dante have a sixth sense when it comes to knowing who is and who isn't a cop. I don't want him running into me when I'm with Tyra.

I was the last person to walk off the plane. I gave Dante plenty of time to exit the terminal. Sign or no sign, I couldn't miss Tyra. She was a beautiful dark complected woman, in her early thirties. She was statuesque, six foot tall in heels, and dressed in a chic creamed colored pantsuit. Her deep-set eyes were complimented by sculptured arched eyebrows, giving her an exotic look. I looked around to make sure that Malatesta wasn't around, before I approached her. I extended my hand and said quietly, "I'm Frank. Just to let you know, one of the bad guys was on the plane with me. I gotta be careful we don't run into him."

"Let's give it some time before we leave the building. By the way, it's nice to meet you. I'm Detective Tyra Williams. Please call me Tyra."

"Tyra it is. Call me Frank. Where to?" She asked if I'd checked a bag, or was the carry on, all I had. "No, this is it."

She tossed her head slightly in the direction that we were going and said in a take charge voice, "My car is parked right in front. Follow me, the team wants meet you."

I kept my eyes peeled, looking for Dante as we walked to her car. We headed for the Metropolitan Police Headquarters in downtown Las Vegas. It's about a twenty-minute drive from the airport. We chatted about our respective departments and made small talk on the drive in. She escorted me to room 301. Tyra got everyone's attention by shouting over the clamor of voices, "Everyone, this is Detective Frank Santorsola from New York!"

They stopped what they were doing, walked over, and introduced themselves to me. Captain Tony Conti walked out of his office. In a welcoming voice, he said, "Frank, it's nice to have you on board. Chief Christopher told me a little bit about your background."

"Captain, Dante Malatesta was on my flight. He's in town."

"Chief Christopher has faxed over his rap sheet."

The captain looked young for his years. Although in his mid forties, he looked ten years younger. Captain Conti asked everyone assigned to the detail to meet in the briefing room. They slowly began to filter out of the squad room and down the hall. Detective Williams had me follow her to room 307. It reminded me of a high school classroom, outfitted with small school type desks. There were twenty or so detectives that took a seat. Detective Williams and I sat next to one another. That was fine with me, I liked looking at her. Captain Conti stood in front of a blackboard that spanned the length of the room. The words, "Operation Computer Gambling," were written in chalk at the top of the board. Tony began the briefing by saying that the Las Vegas Police Department will assist the Westchester County District Attorney's Office in identifying organized crime figures who'll be attending a meeting in the Mirage Hotel and Casino. A Spencer Johnstone, from Fort Worth, will demonstrate a revolutionary computer program that he developed to record illegal gambling wagers. Then, he asked me to stand. "For those of you who haven't met Frank, I'd like to introduce Detective Frank Santorsola. He's from the Westchester County District Attorney's Office, in New York."

I stood and nodded to everyone. Shyly, I quickly sat down. He told everyone that the chief of security at the Mirage Hotel, a former Metro detective, has been able to identify the conference room that the meeting will be held in. The chief of security will also provide us with the names of the people registering at the hotel over the weekend. Captain Conti said, "We'll have a pretty good idea who will be attending the meeting."

Captain Conti called out the names of the detectives, assigning each of them, to one of the four surveillance teams. Their responsibility is to document the movements of the Mafioso during their stay in Vegas. Tony made it a point to tell his detectives to dress like typical guests of the hotel to avoid suspicion. He directed the technical people to install the pin-hole cameras and microphones in the conference room, so that the meeting can be monitored and recorded from a secure room in the basement of the hotel. I raised my hand. "Yes, Frank." Captain Conti said, as he pointed to me. "My office has four teams of detectives surveilling Carmine Corso, 24/7. He seems to be the lynchpin in all of this. So far, he's staying put in New York."

Captain Conti nodded. "For those of you who don't know, Detective Santorsola has been working undercover on a homicide investigation involving the murder of Carmine Corso's son, Gary. Carmine is a Capo in the Genovese crime family, and a very bad man." Captain Conti ended the briefing by saying, "Gambling's not a crime in Las Vegas. You don't have to be a genius to understand why these guys choose Vegas to hold their meeting."

As everyone was getting ready to leave, Tyra leaned over and asked, "Do you have dinner plans tonight? I know a place off the strip that makes the best short ribs, and serves the best Apple Martini's in town."

She didn't have to twist my arm. I leaned back smiling. "I have no plans. What time do we eat?"

She giggled, "Uh, whatever time floats your boat, detective."

I studied her for a moment, not letting on what I was thinking. The woman's stunning, but that's as far as I want to take it. I've got enough problems in my life and didn't need anymore complications. I thought, I'll have dinner and a few drinks, and that'll be the extent of it.

Tyra reached over, smiling. "You must be tired. I'll drive you over to the Mandalay Bay and pick you up at seven thirty."

"Sounds like a plan."

Then it hit me. Clare Iverson danced at that hotel. Like they say, *six degrees of separation*. On our way out, Captain Conti stopped us. He said that once all the gumbas arrive, they'll be photographed. He'd like me to take a look at them to see if Corso is among the group.

I replied, "Absolutely, Cap."

Tyra dropped me off at the hotel where I checked in to a room on the 15th floor, using my fictitious name, Frank Miranda. I couldn't get Clare Iverson off my mind. She once danced at the hotel, and now she's dead. After unpacking what little clothes I had, I decided to go down to the bar for a drink. I had an hour to kill before I met up with Trya.

There was only one vacant seat at the bar. I sat next to a gorgeous young blonde, who was sipping on a glass of white wine. I ordered a Campari and soda and quickly began to relax. I couldn't help but glance at this striking beauty from time to time. She finally looked at me and smiled, and we struck up a conversation. She asked where I was from. She introduced herself as Cat Gardner. I was taken by surprise when she told me that she was a showgirl, who danced in a number of shows on the strip. I thought, Cat had to know Clare Iverson. So I asked, "Do you know Clare Iverson? She's a dancer in Vegas too."

She had a look of disbelief written on her face. "Clare? Yes, I know her. How do you know Clare?"

I wanted to find out all she knew about Clare, so I thought fast and said, "I met her last year in New York. She mentioned that she danced in Vegas. I think she said, here, at Mandalay Bay."

"Wow", she replied, "Clare is spending a lot of time in New York lately. I haven't seen her in a few months. I've been away dancing in Europe and just got back last night."

As delicately as I could put it, I said, "Well, I am sorry to be the bearer of bad tidings but uh…. Clare is dead."

Cat gasped. "Oh my, God. She's dead? What happened?"

"She was murdered. The news was splashed all over the newspapers in New York."

"Who killed her? How? Where? When?"

I looked over at the bartender and asked for another round of drinks, then back at Cat, trying to illicit more information. "They don't know. They haven't found the killer yet."

Cat looked at me like she'd lost her best friend. "Frank, I feel so bad. She was so young and beautiful. She hadn't begun to live her life yet."

"Yes, I know. We were introduced through mutual friends. I was interested in her, but I was told that she was totally wrapped up with somebody. So I backed off."

"She told me her love life had become very complicated. A jealous boyfriend was making her life a living hell. That's all I know. We weren't close friends."

"Really!" I said. "That could prove to be dangerous. The papers said that she was found shot alongside her boyfriend."

"I hope they find her killer."

It was getting late, and it was almost time to meet Tyra. But my chance meeting with Cat Gardner gave me a new angle to pursue in Clare and Gary's death. Perhaps it's a love triangle after all.

CHAPTER TWENTY FOUR

Tyra was waiting in a silver Porsche, at the far end of the portico. I tapped on the window as I opened the door. She said with a grin, "Slide in." Her dark sultry eyes seem to study me as she drove out of the circular driveway into traffic. "I'm taking you to Bon Café. It's off the strip on Paradise Road. The short ribs are to die for, their steaks are aged, and the bartenders can make any drink imaginable."

The Porsche had a standard shift transmission. She effortlessly shifted it into third, then fourth gear on Las Vegas Blvd, obviously enjoying the abundant power the car has. Once off the strip and out into the desert, she accelerated, hitting speeds of 90 to 100 miles an hour. She occasionally looked to see if I had a reaction to her driving at excessive speed, but I really kind of liked it. The Nevada desert is beautiful at dusk. The rocks and mountains are striated with assorted minerals. When the sun hits at the right angle, it reflects off each shade of color, as though you're looking through a kaleidoscope.

In about fifteen minutes, we arrived at the Bon Café. The Café was at one time was an old Spanish Mission, built from red sandstone in 1673 by Spanish priests. A commemorative plaque with the Mission's history is displayed, framed in glass, in the front of the structure. Tyra parked in the parking lot off to one side of the building. She walked around the front of car as I got out. She took my arm, and we walked the short distance into the Mission's lobby. Apparently, she dines here frequently because the smartly attired maître d' greeted her with familiarity. "We've been expecting you. Right this way, Tyra."

He escorted us through a large sandstone archway and into the dining room. We were seated at a table next to a massive stone fireplace. The subtle scent of mesquite faintly filled the room. Our table was dressed in a crisp white tablecloth, fine china, silverware, and crystal wine and water glasses.

Tyra looked gorgeous. She was dressed in a short slim white skirt, knee high white snakeskin boots, a light blue silk blouse, and a pale grey Chanel scarf that was draped around her neck. As for me, I kept it simple.

Jeans, white button down shirt, brown loafers, and a linen blazer. How could I go wrong?

As soon as the waitress came over, Tyra ordered an Apple Vodka Martini. I ordered a glass of Pinot Noir. It wasn't until our second round of drinks arrived that we ordered dinner. Tyra suggested that we try the *Short Ribs Bon Café,* prepared in a reduced Balsamic vinegar sauce, which sounded fine to me. We both ordered it. It was spectacular. As we ate, we kept the conversation light. We were enjoying each others company and the evening seemed to get away from us. We shouldn't have, but we ordered another drink. By now, the both of us were toasted and our conversation became more intimate. I talked about my break-up with Denise and she talked about how hard she had to work to be appointed to the detective division. I complimented Tyra on her exotic looks. Tyra blushed and said, "My mother was born in Egypt and my father was Moroccan. I even have a little Welsh blood in here. I'm a mutt."

"A gorgeous mutt," I replied.

A three-piece band set up in the dining room. They began to play a beautiful Cha-Cha and Tyra grabbed my hand, yanking me up from the table. "Dance with me."

We stared into each other's eyes for a moment. I hesitated but my desire overcame my better judgment. She led me to the dance floor. As we danced, I became enchanted by this Nubian Goddess. She was no stranger to the dance floor. Her body was so erotically in sync with the music that my desire for her overwhelmed me. She clasped her hands behind my neck, while seductively thrusting her hips forward. Her rhythmical movements were more intoxicating then the alcohol I'd been drinking. She closed her eyes, swaying side to side, becoming one with the music. All eyes were on her, including mine. The trio immediately segued into the very seductive song made famous by Latina singer Selena, "I Could Fall in Love." Tyra pulled me closer. We were cheek to cheek. Our sexual tension was palpable. I began to lose myself in the moment and thought about what it would be like to make love to her. I knew we had to stop before things went too far. When the music stopped, I gently guided her back to the table. She excused herself, and headed for the powder room. When she returned, she said, "I can't help but wonder what it would be like if you lived in Las Vegas."

I sighed, "Me too, Tyra."

We gazed silently at one another, each of us lost in thought. I could feel the sexual energy percolating. She leaned across the table, touched my hand and said seductively, "Frank, do you want to come back to my place for a night cap."

I'll admit it. I wanted to go, but I thought better. Transfixed on her beautiful eyes, I shook my head no. "I'd love too, but I don't think it would be wise."

"Frank, you're in love with Denise?"

Looking down into my wine glass and nodding my head, I couldn't hide my feelings. "Yes, I am."

Tyra smiled and said, "She's a lucky woman. Most men would have taken me up on my offer."

I motioned to the waiter for the check and picked up the tab. We listened to music on the ride back to my hotel. Under the hotel portico, I leaned over, took her hand, and kissed it. As I was about to get out of the car, I leaned up against her. "Tyra, I won't forget tonight. You're amazing."

She gently kissed my lips. "You're amazing too. Good night."

The next afternoon, I was still in bed when Captain Conti called and said that the rest of Malatesta's group had arrived on Delta Airlines.

"Frank, Tyra will pick you up in twenty minutes."

"Cap, can you make it thirty minutes, I'm still in bed."

He laughed and said, "Late night, huh?"

It was noon when she arrived. My curiosity about the car was killing me. I had to ask, "Tyra, I gotta ask you. Is the Porsche yours?"

She looked over giggling, as she exited the driveway, heading for the Mirage Hotel. "God, no. It belongs to the department." As she drove around to the service entrance of the hotel, she said, "After this is all over, I want to show you the White Tigers that are suspended in a cage over the casino's floor. They are world famous."

I looked over and winked. "I'd love to get a picture of them."

We entered the building through the service entrance, and walked down the corridor to the Security Control Room. Captain Conti was already there with two detectives. They were putting the final touches on the sound and video equipment.

As soon as he saw us, he waved us over. He took the surveillance photos out of a manila envelope and handed them to me. I studied them, but only recognized Dante Malatesta. As I handed back the photos, he told me that Spencer Johnstone has been spotted in the hotel, and is heading for the conference room. He said their meeting is scheduled to start at 4:00 P.M. It was almost showtime.

A male walked into the room. Captain Conti pointed to the monitor and said, "That's Spencer!" It was exactly four o'clock.

With Spencer, was a hotel staffer pushing a cart loaded with a computer, projector and screen. It wasn't long before Malatesta and the others walked in. Spencer methodically set up the projector and screen. Once in place, Spencer introduced himself to the group, presenting his background in computer science. He then began to show the slides demonstrating his computer program that records the daily wagers of illegal gambling. He highlighted and pointed to the boxes in the program that list the various types of gambling wagers, number bets, and illegal sports bets. He indicated where the bettor's names or code is placed. Spencer showed them spaces for the runners name, the money wagered, and commissions earned by each runner. Two boxes list the daily winners and losers. And at the end of the spreadsheet, there's a box for the profits and the losses. He emphasized that traditionally illegal bets are written on paper which are subject to seizure by the police. He explained that instead of the clerk taking the bets and writing them down, he'd enter the information via the computer onto the spread sheet, storing them until he's ready to send them to a secure location for tabulation. He explained that the genius of his program is that insulates the wire room operators from arrest and prosecution. Spencer was demonstrative, gesturing with his hands as he spoke. He ended by saying that it is a win-win situation for illegal gambling. He then introduced Captain Hugo Zapata-Feliz of the Mexican Federal Police who will provide protection for the operation in Mexico City.

It was about 6:00 P.M when the group of Mafioso slowly got up and began to leave the room. Malatesta walked over to Spencer, whispering something that the microphones couldn't pick up. By the look on Johnstone's face, we felt that the meeting didn't go well. You could see it by the scowl on his face, as he and Malatesta walked out.

Captain Conti suggested that Tyra and I grab a bite to eat before meeting him back at headquarters for a debriefing in two hours. Tyra suggested that we try Emeril's Delmonico restaurant in the Venetian Hotel. Me, I've always wanted to dine in one of Chef Emeril Lagasse's restaurants. Friends of mine ate at "Emeril's" his flagship restaurant in New Orleans. They said that the food was outrageously good. They were right. We had an extraordinary meal of the most delicious bone-in-rib eye steaks. During our meal, we had much less to drink than we did last night, and purposely kept our conversation light, staying away from personal stuff. After dinner, we headed back to the police department, meeting up with Captain Conti and the rest of the detectives assigned to the detail, in their conference room.

Captain Conti read a report, listing the names of the Mafioso who attended the meeting. I was quite impressed. Mafiosi from all parts of the country came together like a big corporation. There was Lucchese soldier, Johnny "Socks" La Torre, from Brooklyn, "Little Nicky Nardi," from Philadelphia, who represented the Bonnano's, John Salerno, from Chicago, "Joe the Nose" Vitti, a Colombo soldier from New Jersey, and Dante Malatesta, who put the meeting together. They had lengthy arrest records for illegal gambling, loan sharking, extortion, assault, truck high-jacking, and mortgage fraud. Some of them had been suspects in a number of contract killings. This meeting was reminiscent of the Appalachin meeting of 1957. It was a meeting of high ranking Mafiosi, who were busted at Joseph Barbara's stone mansion, in upstate New York, as they discussed their criminal enterprise. The Appalachin meeting provided a wealth of intelligence for the entire law enforcement community. It truly demonstrated that crime families are connected and met in secret to discuss their criminal interests. On that day in history, the FBI finally had to admit that the Mafia existed.

After the debriefing, Captain Conti and a few of his detectives took me out for a few drinks at their favorite watering hole. Tyra chose not to come. We both knew that we had feelings for one another, so perhaps she felt awkward. I flew back to New York the next morning, but not before Tyra took me back to the Mirage, where I took a few pictures of the magnificent White Tigers, suspended in a cage over the casino.

CHAPTER TWENTY FIVE

My flight landed at Kennedy Airport at1:30 P.M. I was met at the American Airlines gate by one of the squad detectives who drove me home. I'd planned to call Chief Christopher, give him a quick update on the happenings in Vegas, and then take the rest of the day off. After the six-hour flight and the time zone change, I was beat.

I got out of the car, put my bag down on the side walk, and thanked the detective for the ride. From the corner of my eye, I noticed a late model black Cadillac parked a few hundred feet down the street. As the detective pulled into traffic, the Cadillac slowly pulled out from the curb, towards me. I followed the Cadillac as it continued slowly up the street. As I bent down to pick up my bag, the passenger side window of the car slid down. I looked up and saw a white male point a pistol out of the window at me. My senses suddenly kicked in to overdrive. I felt the rush of adrenaline and the terrifying fear of being killed. The guy pointing the gun at me was the same guy who shot Nutsey in Rye and attempted to kill me. I reacted instinctively, threw myself to the ground, rolling over and over, towards a small row of hedges in front of the building. I heard at least four gun shots. Bang, Bang, Bang, Bang! It happened so quickly, I didn't have time to think. The next thing I heard was car tires screeching as he sped away. Shaken, I slowly got up, brushed the dirt off me, and made sure that I wasn't hit. I looked to see if anyone was on the street who might have witnessed the shooting. The street was quiet, there was no one around. I slowly picked up my bag, entered the building, thinking as I open my apartment door that I must be pushing somebody's buttons hard. They want me dead.

I immediately called the chief's office. His secretary answered. I must have sounded upset, so she rushed to find him. A split second later he picked up. I told him that I'd just been shot at and I believed it's the same person who tried to kill me in Rye. Needless to say he was upset and asked if I was okay.

"Frankie, I'll send as few guys over to keep you company!"

I thought about it for a second and said, "No thanks Chief, it won't be necessary. I can take care of myself."

He paused for a second and said, "Frank, are you sure you don't want me to send someone over?"

"I'm sure chief, thanks."

I needed to take the edge off. I picked up the bottle of Blanton's Bourbon, and poured myself a stiff drink, quickly knocking it back. I poured another glass, throwing it down as fast as the first one. I was tired and needless to say, upset. I hadn't eaten anything but the few bags of peanuts they give you on the plane. I just wasn't hungry, and decided that the best thing I could do was to get some sleep. But, sleep wouldn't come. I kept tossing and turning all night, picturing the face of the man who tried to kill me. I needed to resolve this situation, and fast.

CHAPTER TWENTY SIX

The next morning Chief Christopher was standing in the hallway outside my office waiting for me to arrive. He was agitated and clearly upset. His voice rose in frustration. "Frank we are going to get these guys. I'm pulling out all the stops. We're talking to our informants and I even called the local FBI. Something's gotta pop. We'll find them."

"Chief, I have no doubt that we're going to find these scumbags. They'd better hope that I don't find them first."

He didn't say a thing and quickly moved the conversation to Spencer Johnstone and Dante Malatesta. "Um, well, you'll be interested in this. We just intercepted a call from Johnstone. Spencer tells Malatesta that Patrick Johns hasn't arrived with the scheduled delivery of money. He was supposed to get there last night with five hundred thousand dollars."

He went on to tell me that Malatesta went crazy over the phone. He said that he could be heard violently cursing Johns. He told Spencer that he wants Johns to call him as soon as he gets there. According to the chief, Spencer mumbled something and quickly changed the subject asking why Malatesta's friends weren't interested in his computerized gambling program. The chief said that Malatesta didn't beat around the bush and gave a blunt answer. "These guys are old time Mustache Pete's. They're set in their ways, and don't like change. They couldn't agree among themselves, so they chucked the idea."

Johnstone huffed, "Damn it!" Then said, "When these guys get ready to enter the 21st century, let me know."

The chief said that Malatesta could be heard in the apartment seething because Johns hadn't arrived with the money yet. He's heard telling his uncle that he should have Johns tied to a cactus in the desert and shot. He immediately called Johnstone back and told him to call him as soon as Johns got there. Malatesta called Wayne's house every hour on the hour. It got so bad Wayne finally stopped answering his phone.

By late afternoon, Johns still hadn't gotten to Johnstone's house with the money. At about 4:00 P.M. Malatesta left his uncle's building in a huff, and was followed by the surveillance team to Corso's yard in New Rochelle. Corso had consolidated both of his companies at the New Rochelle yard. According to the surveillance team, Carmine was in the yard pacing backing back and forth in an agitated state. Malatesta drove erratically into the yard slamming on the breaks. He jumped out of the car, and ran up to Carmine. They were eye to eye, and agitated. After a minute or so, they took their conversation out onto the sidewalk. They spoke for about five minutes, when Malatesta abruptly walked back into the yard, got into his car, and drove out of the yard, tires screeching. The team took him directly back to his uncles house, where he was overheard on the bug telling his uncle that when he gets his hands on Johns, he's gonna rip his heart out and feed it to his pigs.

He remained in the apartment for about thirty minutes. After lighting up a cigarette in front of the building, he jumped into his Mercedes, and was followed to the same social club he's known to frequent off Westchester Square in the Bronx. He stayed in the club until 11P.M., and was then followed home where he remained for the rest of the night.

CHAPTER TWENTY SEVEN

The next day I was back at it, reviewing tapes. What I wanted was to get back on the street and look for the free-holes who were trying to kill me. From what I'm being told, the guys assigned to find them aren't having much luck. Since the last incident, I'm on edge all the time, constantly looking over my shoulder. I feel like my head is on a swivel, looking for the bastards to show up. I have to be extremely careful when leaving the office, and especially around my apartment. In a way, I'm glad that Denise isn't living with me. That's one less thing I have to worry about.

Detective Achim called me from the wire room and said that the chief wanted to see me. I asked him why, he said he didn't know. When I walked into the wire room, Andrei and the chief were excited. Larry immediately said, "Frankie, the wire is heating up. I need you here." Andrei glanced up at the chief, and tapped him on his arm to get his attention. Andrei, usually reserved, was excited. He looked at the chief, and then at me and said, "Frankie, you're going to like this. I just recorded another volatile conversation between Dante and Spencer Johnstone."

"What, what's goin on?"

Andrei said he took the tape off the bug had it duplicated so I could listen to it. The particular conversation they were keying in on was between Malatesta and Johnstone. "Cheech, the chief wants you to hear it." Andrei hit the play button on the recorder. Malatesta is heard ranting ferociously. "That mother fucker disappeared with our money! There's nowhere that cockroach can hide that we can't find him!"

"So what ya gonna do?"

Malatesta screams into the phone, "I'll tell ya what I'm gonna do, I'm gonna make an example of him! I'm gonna have his hands chopped off and stuck up his ass. Then I'm going to gut him like a pig!" Malatesta slammed the phone down, leaving Spencer on the line.

As Spencer is hanging up, he's heard muttering, "Oh, fuck."

I snapped, "Shit it looks like Johns stole $500,000, and is on the run."

Both Andrei and the chief nodded their head in agreement. Then the chief said, "It certainly looks that way."

We were glued to the monitors. Malatesta is heard making muted sounds in the background. We didn't have to wait long. Malatesta blurted out over the living room bug, shouting to his Uncle Dominick. "Dom, can that private investigator be trusted?"

His uncle, apparently in another room, yelled back, "Do you mean Jack Shaw, the ex NYPD cop? The one who does us favors?"

Malatesta stammers as if he's trying to remember the guy's name. "Yeah, a ---- him. I need his phone number."

Footsteps are heard walking around the room. From a distance, his uncle is heard shouting, "I'll get his number. I'll be right back."

A long moment passed. His uncle walked back into the room. Malatesta then dials out. The number he called is listed to Jack Shaw, 2526 Corbett Road, Bronx, NY, a private house. Shaw answers the phone business like, "J &S Investigations, Jack speaking."

"Jack, this is Dante. I got a situation." Dante tells Shaw that a money courier has run off with five hundred thousand dollars of family money, and he wants him found. Dante sounds exasperated over the phone, and asks Shaw, "Can you find him for us?"

Shaw replied confidently, "No problem, I can find him, but it will cost you."

Malatesta was furious about Shaw's response. He mumbled something, then said, "Don't worry about the fucking money! You'll get every fucking penny that's coming to you!"

Shaw was stunned, replying sharply, "I want ten thousand up front and ten thousand on the back end, when I find him."

Malatesta grunted, "My Uncle Dom will bring over the ten large. There better be no mistakes and don't write anything down about our arrangement. You got it."

Shaw's edginess was obvious. "I understand completely. Believe me. Have faith."

A female's voice is heard entering the room. "Dante, can I make you coffee?"

Dante shouts, "Not now. Can't you see I'm on the phone?"

Shaw continues, "Fine, Dante. What I'll need is the guy's name and cell phone number to track him. I got a friend in AT &T. He'll be able to track him from his calls. We'll find out where he's calling from, pinpointing his location. As soon as I have the information and the ten grand, I'll start the ball rolling."

"Enough with the fucking money. You'll get it! My Uncle Dom will bring everything you need."

We stood there transfixed on what we just heard. The money laundering case was about to unfold before our eyes and ears. It looked like Patrick Johns was on the run with five hundred thousand dollars of mob money. We knew what our next move had to be, we had to get a wire up on Jack Shaw's phone as fast as we could. We needed to find Johns before Malatesta did. We now have a moral obligation to save his life. Chief Christopher bolted out of the room, heading directly to Hogan's office. Hogan needed to act quickly, have the wiretap order drawn up, and have a judge sign it.

Just then, Denise called. Whoa, I stiffened up, caught completely by surprise. I had to take a moment and catch my breath before answering. She didn't give me a chance to say hello. She asked with an urgent voice, "Frankie, are you able to talk?" I told her no. I'd call her right back.

I headed for my office like a horse with blinders on. My heart was pounding a mile a minute. A few of the guys tried to get my attention on the way to my office, but I brushed past them. I dialed Denise's number.

I could tell from the sound of her voice that she was anxious. "Hey Frankie, how are you?"

I tried to gain my composure, but I couldn't. I missed the hell out of her. "How am I? You're on my mind every freaking minute of the day."

She broke down and began to cry. "Me too, I made a big mistake walking out on you. I can't sleep, I can't work. I'm wondering what you're doing every minute of the day, and if you're okay. Frankie, I've been doing a lot of thinking about us. I want us to be together, no matter what. I'm hoping that you feel the same."

My throat muscles tightened. Finally, I was able to force the words out. I knew I needed to be honest and up front with her. I paused for a second to gather my thoughts. "I've been doing a lot of thinking too, and what I want most of all, is for us to be together."

Denise's sighed. "Me too."

"There's more. Please let me finish. You have to know that I won't always be able to talk about what my day was like. Sometimes it's not ethical, and sometimes, I just can't bring myself to speak about it. At times, it's too hard for me. I know that you know that I want us to be together, now, more than ever, but I need to know that you accept me as I am. I'm a cop. It's what I do."

Denise was still sobbing. "I know, I know. I love you and that's all that matters. I want us to be together. During our time apart, I've been doing a lot of soul searching, and I know that I'll be strong enough to handle my fear of losing you. Frankie, I love you." A long moment passed. Then Denise said softly, "I want to come home."

At that moment, I wished she could. Reluctantly, I had to tell her that something was going on right now, and she needed to stay away from the apartment for a while. I'd explain it to her when I could. She needed to trust me. There was a longing in my voice. "Honey, I'll pick you up tonight. We can spend sometime together, but I really have to be careful. Where can I meet you?"

My girlfriend lives in Larchmont. I'll take the 6:15 P.M. train. It gets into the station at 6:42 P.M."

"Okay. See ya then."

The time seemed to stand still. I tried to occupy myself in the office, but all I could do was watch the clock. A few of the guys even commented, and asked me if everything was okay. Finally it was time to leave the office and pick her up in Larchmont. I was still driving that old beat up Cadillac, but who cared. I was getting back together with the love of my life.

She was standing on the platform when I drove into the station plaza. She took my breath away. When she saw me she waved and ran down the platform steps and to the car. I was barely out of the car when she put her arms around me, almost knocking me off my feet. She reached for my face, gently kissing my lips. Between kisses she quietly mouthed, "I love you," over and over again. A number of commuters stared at us as they walked by.

Being together again brought me to another time and place. I remembered the first time we kissed, the first time we made love. She slowly pushed herself away and said seductively, "Let's go somewhere quiet for dinner. Frankie, we have a lot of catching up to do."

CHAPTER TWENTY EIGHT

The District Attorney wasted no time having a wiretap order signed and a tap placed on Jack Shaw's phone. The wire room was so crowded with cops and eavesdropping equipment you could hardly move. The guys monitoring the phones and bug had to wear headphones to listen in and record the pertinent conversations. The wiretap on Shaw's phone produced positive results right off the bat. Malatesta asked Shaw if his uncle had dropped off the money.

Shaw replied with a Bronx Irish brogue, "Yeah, he dropped it off thirty minutes ago. Thanks."

Malatesta growled, "Make sure that you call me right away if you get something. If I'm not here, my Uncle Dom knows how to get me."

Shaw replied, "Got it."

Shaw, a big husky Irishman born in Shannon, Ireland, retired from the New York City Police Department a few years ago at age fifty. The Intel guys obtained some background information on Shaw from their contacts in NYPD's Internal Affairs Bureau. Shaw retired as a first grade detective, spending most of his career as a squad detective in the 46th precinct in the Bronx. He had an exemplary record, retired and went into private security. Internal Affairs faxed over his personal history and physical description. Shaw is licensed to carry a firearm. He owns a Smith & Wesson, 357 model 19, handgun. His New York City pistol permit number is 008972. We'll have to keep this in mind when it comes to dealing with the guy.

It was about 11:00 A.M. when I walked into the wire room to find out firsthand what was going on. Dante Malatesta had just hung up from a call with Jack Shaw. There was a buzz in the room about Malatesta's conversation with Shaw. Detective Achim filled me in and it seemed that things were getting to a boiling point in the investigation. Just then a dial tone was heard on Shaw's phone, digits on his phone were being pressed as Shaw dialed out to a 212 area code in New York City. Everyone in the plant took their headphones off to listen to the call. The phone rang twice and it was answered by a male on the other end of the call. "AT & T Security. Mitch Humphrey speaking."

"Mitch, Jack Shaw."

Mitch replied, "Jack, I'll call you back on a private line." Moments later he called Jack back. "Hey Jack, what's up?"

"I need to track a cell phone number. Friends of mine want to find this guy."

"Sure, Jack. Give me the number."

Shaw replied, "Hum, it's 718-555-2020."

Humphrey asks, "Who is the phone listed to?"

"Patrick Johns."

"Okay, I'll pull his phone records and see where he's calling from. It's my usual fee, right?" Humphrey said as if wanting to make sure they had an understanding.

Shaw replied, "Absolutely," and hung up.

Chief Christopher called. "Frank, I tried your office first."

"Hey Chief, what's up?"

I could tell by the tone of his voice that he was pumped. "I just got off the phone with the White Plains FBI. One of their informants was drinking at a bar in Brooklyn. He met two guys at the bar who were three sheets to the wind. Their conversation digressed to a tale of a contract hit on a Westchester cop that they were having trouble fulfilling. It was making the guy who hired them angry and he's not one to make angry. The informant tried to get the cops name, but they wouldn't give it up."

"Well, we can guess who the cop is."

Christopher huffed, "Frank, the C.I. is friendly with the owner of the bar and the owner knows who these guys are. The Bureau is adamant that these animals are dealt with somewhere other than the bar, in order to protect the informant, and the bar owner. The C.I. got their names and we'll find out where they hang their hats."

I gruffly asked, "Who are they? Who do they work for?"

"Interpol indicated that the shooter was most likely Gennaro Balistrieri and the driver of the car, Anton Cermack. They are from the Czech Republic. Cermack has a lengthy criminal record in the Czech Republic for assault, extortion, rape, and attempted murder. Somehow he has made it into the United States. Balistrieri is said to be a sadist and brutal hit man, who has allegedly added several women to his list of kills. He's never been arrested or prosecuted for any of his crimes. Frank, they're killers for hire, and it looks like we'll take them off the street soon."

The thought of finally arresting them seemed to calm me. "Chief, does the FBI know who hired them?"

"No, Frank. They don't know yet, but their guy has his ear to the ground. If he hears anything he'll call the Bureau immediately, and they'll take it from there."

"Is that right? But I want to be there. I owe them. I want to be the one who puts the cuffs on them."

There was angst in the chief's voice. "I don't think it would be a good idea, but we'll see how it shakes out."

Andrei called and asked me to hurry back into the wire room. He said that Malatesta had just received a call from Jack Shaw who said that his guy in the phone company had just gotten back to him. He said that after pulling Johns' toll records, Johns' last call was made from Montvale, New Jersey. Malatesta told Shaw that he would find out who Johns knows in New Jersey and get back to him. The chief and I walked in as Malatesta could be overheard on the bug talking to his Uncle. We listened with baited breath. Malatesta asked his uncle, "Uncle Dom, didn't Johns' say that he has a son who lives in New Jersey?"

199

"Yeah, why?"

Malatesta is heard breathing hard as he spit out, "I just got off the phone with Shaw. He said that Johns' last call was made from Montvale, New Jersey. Do me a favor and have Pete Esposito stop up."

"I'll call him now."

Malatesta picks up the house phone and dialed out. He punched in Shaw's number. Shaw picked up right away. "Jack Shaw."

"Jack, its Dante."

Shaw put another call on hold. "What do you got, Dante?"

Malatesta raised his voice. His voice booming over the phone. "Johns' son lives in Montvale. Can you get me his address right away?"

Shaw sounded a little uncertain. "If the kid's last name is Johns, I should have it for you shortly."

Malatesta shouted into the phone, "Call me as soon as you get it!" and hung up.

Chief Christopher in a hurried voice said, "Frank, I want you and Nulligan on the street right away. You need to get to Johns' son before they do. As soon as we get the son's address we'll call you. We've got to get to Johns' before Malatesta does." I looked at him knowing exactly what he meant. "Frank, take the Firebird." He turned to Andrei. "Andrei, get a hold of Joe. Tell him to meet Frank on North Broadway at the I-287 entrance ramp. Frank will brief him there."

Andrei sat straight up in his swivel chair, turning towards the chief and replied, "Yes, sir."

I grabbed my sawed-off shotgun, two bullet proof vests, and ran out of the squad room. Before I reached my car, my cell phone rang. "Hey Cheech, what's going on? Andrei told me to get my ass in gear ASAP and meet you on North Broadway by exit 6!"

I was about to brief Joe when I got another call. I put Joe on hold. It was Andrei. Excitedly, he said, "Frank, Malatesta was just overheard talking to someone by the name of Pete about Patrick Johns. He told Pete that he's waiting for a call back from Jack Shaw. Malatesta says that Johns' last cell call was from Montvale, New Jersey. He thinks that's where Johns' is holed up. As soon as he gets his son's address, he wants Pete to take a ride."

"Andrei, I got Joe on hold."

"Frank, Malatesta is telling Pete, 'You know what to do. For his sake, I hope the motherfucker is alone. If he's not, everyone with him goes. Understand? I want the fucking money back. I want you to send a message. Cut his hands off and take them with you. I want the fucking thief buried without his hands. Capisci?'

Andrei mumbled into the phone, "It sounds like Dante is talking to Pete Esposito. Esposito says that he understands, and asks Dante if Johns is the guy they met with in the social club in Westchester Square?"

"Andrei, anything else?"

Hang on, "Yeah, he's telling Pete that that's him. Johns is driving a grey Lincoln Town car."

"Andrei, I gotta get back to Joe."

Joe had hung up.

I called Andrei and told him that I wanted a criminal history and a physical description of Esposito, so we know who and what we're dealing with. "I have it right here." He said that Esposito is a documented associate of the Genovese crime family. *There is a difference between an associate and a made man. A made man is referred to as a solider or solider button. He has been formally inducted into one of the organized crime families by a blood ceremony. Be it a made man or an associate, they all honor the Mafia's code of silence, called Omerta. When a soldier or an associate is ordered to kill, he can't refuse.*

Although Esposito is baby faced with puffy round rosy cheeks, he is an intimidating figure. He looks like he has ice running through his veins. His most distinctive feature is the serrated-like scar over his left eye that he likely received while making a name for himself on the street. Esposito is a career criminal with a lengthy rap sheet going back to his teenage years. In 1978, he was arrested for petit larceny of meat stolen from an A&P in the Bronx. As an adult, he's been arrested for violating New York State gambling laws, armed robbery, burglary, aggravated assault with a deadly weapon, and for driving a high-jacked truck carrying only men's left shoes. It was a common practice in the 1980's for manufacturers to ship left or right shoes separately making the cargo useless and thus discouraging high-jackers. Dante spent three years in Sing-Sing Prison for the truck high-jacking. He was arrested again in 2002 for the theft of a bulldozer from a Manhattan construction sight. Peter Esposito has been married to Bonnie, nee Marciano, age thirty-seven, since 1996. They have no children. They've been living at 2717 Lurting Avenue, Bronx, NY for the last five years.

Andrei said, Dante, his uncle and Pete Esposito must have walked out of the living room. Their conversation over the bug became barely audible.

Joe pulled up behind me, parking his Crown Victoria on North Broadway. He opened my passenger side door and slid in beside me. He looked over and said, "Frankie, I hope you ate your Wheaties today."

Andrei had pulled up Johns' address on the internet. We had it at the same time Dante received it. At exactly 2:15 P.M. the phone rang in the uncle's apartment. His Uncle Dom answered the call. Jack Shaw gave the uncle's Johns' son's address, 205 Allendale Road in Montvale. The house number is listed to Robert Johns, 201-444-6666.

They must have walked back into the living room. Andrei shouted into the phone, "Esposito is leaving! Shaw is going to let Dante know if Johns moves to another location."

We needed to know what car Esposito is driving. Joe called Angel, who was sitting on the uncle's apartment, and briefly told him what was going down. He told Angel that one of Malatesta henchmen is on his way to kill Patrick Johns, who's at his son's house in Montvale, New Jersey. We need to know what make of car he's driving. Angel shot back, "Joey, a guy just walked out of the building. He seems to be in a hurry. He's getting into a late model black Chrysler, with New York registration BHC 9087. He's pulling away now."

"Thanks Angel. I gotta go."

Joe immediately called the office for a Department of Motor Vehicles (DMV) listing on NY Registration BHC 9087. In a matter of minutes, the car came back registered to Peter Esposito.

I asked Joe to drive, and tossed him the keys to the Firebird. The fucking car is a relic. It's a two door, has bucket seats, and is painted black except for the gold eagle embossed on the hood. Joe burned rubber, speeding onto I-287. We didn't talk much as Joe raced westbound, towards the Tappan Zee Bridge, and onto I-87 North. I don't know about Joe, but I was thinking about Esposito, and if he decided to go the hard way. I checked the shotgun to make sure that it was loaded. Joe mumbled something under his breath. I looked at him with an expression on my face like, what the fuck did you just say?

He glanced over, shrugging his shoulders slightly. "I guess Christopher will give the local police a heads up."

I replied excitedly, "I hope so."

Joe's eyes never left the road. Suddenly, he said, "Um, I think we take exit 13S to the Palisades Parkway South into New Jersey?"

Focusing on the GPS affixed to the dash, I quickly replied. "Yeah, after that, the GPS indicates we exit at 8W and take Route 59W towards Spring Valley. I guess it's a short cut to Montvale."

We were hitting speeds of over ninety miles an hour. My eyes were riveted on the road; every muscle in my body was tense. Joe's voice choked as he said, "Okay, let me know where we turn after that."

"Sure," I said, "The GPS gives an ETA of fifteen minutes." At that moment, we heard a siren behind us.

Joe looked in the rear view mirror and saw flashing red lights and yelled, "Oh, shit! There's a trooper behind us!"

"Just keep going!"

The trooper's car was on our bumper. Over his loud speaker we could hear him clearly, "Pull your car over on the shoulder! Pull it over, now!"

We had no choice. We slowed down, coming to a stop on the shoulder of the road. The trooper pulled up behind us. He slowly got out of his car and approached our car with his gun drawn. Joe and I sat there holding our shields out of the window. All I could think about was getting to the house before Esposito got there. The trooper stood behind the driver's side door. "Let me see your other hands!" The trooper grabbed Joe's police identification and studied it for a split second. Breathing hard he said, "Why didn't you pull over when you saw me chasing you?"

Joe impatiently explained the situation as quickly as he could. Then he put the dome light on the roof of the car as the trooper handed him back his ID. He asked us if we wanted him to follow us to the house. We shouted, "No, thanks," as we peeled out, off the shoulder.

As we approached the house, Esposito flew past us. "Joe, that's Esposito! Stay behind him!"

There was no time to put on our vests or to think about a game plan. We just had to stop Esposito from hurting Johns. We sped down Allendale Avenue, and screeched to a stop behind Esposito's car. He had parked a few houses south of Johns' son's house. He was about fifty feet in front of us, walking towards the house at a fast gait. With not a moment to lose, Joe and I sprung out of the car like a well oiled machine, and onto the sidewalk. I don't think our feet hit the ground. Nulligan drew his .45

caliber Browning, as I clenched the 12 gauge. Esposito was almost at the front door by the time we reached him. He must have heard us coming, because he turned around with a startled look. His threatening eyes fired through on us as we rushed him. "Esposito, police! Police! Get down on the ground!"

Esposito scowled, he threw back his jacket, drew a small caliber handgun from his waistband, and hollered, "Fuck you! Fuck you guys!"

It was a split second decision for the both of us. We knew that he was going to try to kill us. We opened up on him, lighting him up like a fucking Christmas tree. As the double 0 buck and .45 caliber rounds hit him from six feet away, he was blown out of his shoes. He landed on the front steps on his back. Joe and I ran up to him. His eyes blank, his mouth was wide open, as blood poured out and onto the pavement. I saw him take his last breath as his body went limp. He was dead. This is what fucking nightmares are made of.

Suddenly the front door opened and a man in his forties poked his head out, pleading for us not to shoot. He said, "My father's in the basement. He wants to surrender!"

Someone must have called the local police. Sirens were heard off in the distance. Joe and I were wired as our adrenalin rush put us on high alert. We were ready for bear, and didn't know what to expect when we confronted Patrick Johns. Nulligan shouted, "Take us to the basement! Now!"

Johns' son Robert, nervously said, "Ca-ca-come, follow me."

He walked us through the living room where his wife and two small kids cowered in fear, behind the sofa. Robert's legs didn't seem to want to move as fast Joe wanted him to move, so Joe shoved him into the kitchen. Robert raised his finger pointing to the basement door, pausing for a second. "My father's down stairs. Please don't hurt him, he's sick."

Joe and I rushed for the door, cautiously opening it. The basement was lit up. Guns drawn, we slowly walked down the cellar steps. Johns was leaning on a pool table with his hands in the air as we inched our way towards him. On the pool table lay a .38 caliber pistol and a .308 caliber Remington rifle. Joe spun him around, jacked his arms behind his back and cuffed him. Johns muttered a muffled "Ouch."

Joe pushed him down, bending him forward onto the table, and began to go through his pockets, searching around his waist for more weapons. All he found was a bottle of prescription medicine. Joe asked, "Are you Patrick Johns?"

He nodded and said, "Yes, I am."

I began to read him his Miranda Rights, as we heard the pounding of footsteps on the stairs followed by raucous shouts of "Police! Police! Freeze!" A half dozen uniformed cops landed at the bottom of the steps with their guns drawn. Joe and I held our shields high in the air. One of the uniformed officers radioed his sergeant. In a matter of minutes, a large man, with a milk white complexion, walked down the cellar steps. He had three gold stripes on his sergeant's uniform. As calmly as I could, I told him that we assumed that his department was going to be notified by our department.

His face, red with rage, screamed, "We weren't notified! If we were, the guy on the steps might not be dead." Joe, trying to be diplomatic, said, "Sorry, we were running at ninety miles an hour. We didn't have time to call. I guess wires got crossed."

We took Johns over to a corner of the basement and briefed him on why we were there and why there was a body lying outside the front door. Several calls were then made between the two agencies to smooth things over. Eventually, we walked out of the house with Johns, and his small arsenal of weapons. His son and daughter-in-law looked on as we put him in the back of the Firebird. As we pulled away, Johns looked through the rear window as the Bergen County Medical Examiner was zipping up Esposito in a body bag. I remember him turning away from the house, taking what appeared to be a deep sigh of relief.

It wouldn't be long before Dante found out what happened and realized that we were onto him. Now with Johns in custody, we might be in a position to find out a lot more about Malatesta and Carmine Corso.

CHAPTER TWENTY NINE

I couldn't help but wonder what Johns did with the half million dollars. I'm sure we'll find out. I called the chief and told him that we were on our way. He wanted us to take him directly to the interrogation room. Zack would be waiting for us. On the ride to the Court House, Joe, in his usual gruff manor, asked rhetorically, "Is all this shit worth it? I'd really like to fucking know."

Johns' looked like a beaten man. He was slumped back in the seat, and didn't answer him. When we arrived back at the office, Johns seemed to be out of breath; he was breathing hard. We quickly got him out of the car and into the elevator. He leaned on the rear wall of the elevator, silent, and staring down at the floor on our ride to the fourth floor. On our way to the interrogation room, Patrick abruptly stopped, and asked for a favor. "Guys, could I get a glass of water? I'm thirsty, plus I got to take my pills."

His hopeless demeanor must have struck a cord with Joe, as Joe replied, "Sure Pat. I'll get you water as soon as we get into the room."

Zack was already there when we walked in. He studied Johns for a moment, and told him to take a seat. Joe put his hand on Johns' shoulder pushing him down into the chair, then securing his ankles with shackles. Joe calmly said, "I'll get your water now."

Zack introduced himself. "I'm Assistant District Attorney Zack Friedman. I'll be questioning you."

I took a seat at the far end of the table and told Johns that the interview would be video recorded. John's nervously tapped his hand on the table and asked if it was okay to smoke. Zack nodded yes.

In a matter of minutes Joe walked back into the room carrying a small bottle of water. Pat took a hefty swig and asked for his medicine. Zack looked at Joe shrugging his shoulders. "Medicine, what medicine?"

Joe raised his eyebrows and said, "He takes some kind of prescription medication."

Johns, his voice breaking asked, "Mr. Friedman, I need to take my medicine. I have a heart condition."

Zack asked Joe to get Mr. Johns an ashtray, and give him his medication.

Joe reached into his shirt pocket and pulled out the bottle of prescription medicine, handing it to Pat. He then slid an ashtray in front of Johns.

Johns pulled a pack of Marlboro's from his tee shirt pocket and took out a cigarette, but realized he didn't have matches. "I need matches."

Reluctantly, I replied, "Pat, I'll get you matches."

This was a good time to call Denise and let her know that I was alright. She answered right away. "I knew it was you, darling." I reassured her that I was thinking about her, and that I was okay. I told her that I'd call her later. I grabbed a book of matches from one of the desks, and re-entered the interrogation room. Zack and Joe looked extremely anxious. I wondered what I missed. Zack looked across the table and said, "Mr. Johns, Detective Santorsola is going to read you your Constitutional Rights."

I looked directly at Pat as I turned on the video recorder. He suddenly got a burst of energy and became belligerent. "So read me my fucking rights and get it over with."

I read him his rights for the record, and then the questioning began. Immediately, Zack went for the jugular. "If it wasn't for these detectives you and your family would be dead right now. I hope that you realize that?"

Patrick picked up the bottle of water, took another sip, and said, "I knew they'd be coming after me, but I thought I'd have more time."

We were puzzled by what he said. "More time for what?" Joe barked.

Johns sighed, "Time to give my family the money, the money I took from Dante."

We knew that Johns was at the end of his rope and we were the only ones who could help him. Zack reached across the table and grabbed Pat's arm. "Pat, as it stands, you will be charged with money laundering, as will Dante Malatesta, and Spencer Johnstone. You can be smart and cooperate. Why don't you help yourself?"

Pat took a long breath as he thought about what Zack had just said.

At that moment, Chief Christopher called my phone. "Please excuse me, I need to take this call." I stepped out of the room for a moment. Larry didn't waste any time, getting right to the point. "Frank, sorry to interrupt, but I just got a call from the FBI. Gennaro Balistrieri and Anton Cermack were found shot to death in a Brooklyn apartment. It looks like somebody wanted them dead."

"I didn't expect to hear that chief. Someone got to them before we did."

"Frank, it looks that way."

When I re-entered the room, Johns was nervously tapping his pack of cigarettes on the table.

From the look on my face Joe and Zack knew that something was wrong. Joe asked, "Frankie, everything okay?"

'Yeah fine. Let's get on with this."

Suddenly Pat spoke up, surprising everyone. "Uh, I'll testify against all of them, but I want a lawyer before I say anything. I'll lay the whole thing out for you." Zack turned video recorder off and asked Johns if he knew an attorney. "Yes," he replied. "Andrew Cullen."

Zack slid Johns the phone. Johns called Cullen's office. It was getting late, but Cullen was still working. Pat told him that he's been arrested and is facing heavy time. He wanted to dig himself out by cooperating with the DA's office. Cullen told him to hold tight. He'd be at the Court House in a half an hour.

We sat there waiting for Cullen to arrive. He was late, and didn't walk into the interview room until 6:30 P.M. He asked if could have some time alone with his client. We left the room and waited twenty minutes before Cullen walked out into the hallway, and said that his client would be willing cooperate, but only if he's given some assurances.

Zack responded, "We'll have to see what he can give us before we make any deals. Let's hear what he has to say."

Cullen sat next to Pat as Zack turned the video recorder on. Zack said in a commanding voice, "Mr. Cullen, your client has been read his rights. It's my understanding that he would like to waive his rights and cooperate with the District Attorney's Office. He was arrested earlier today and charged with money laundering. I'm sure that your client has told you that he works for Dante Malatesta, transporting mob money. Apparently, he ran off with five hundred thousand dollars of their money. We have reliable information that Malatesta ordered Peter Esposito to find your client, torture him, get the money back, and then kill him. Detectives Santorsola and Nulligan intervened, rescuing your client from Esposito's clutches. Unfortunately, to do that, they were forced to shoot and kill Mr. Esposito in the process."

"Yes, Mr. Friedman, my client has advised me of what has transpired, and is willing to cooperate, if his demands are met."

Zack looked directly at Andrew Cullen and said, "What can he give us and what does he want?"

Johns looked at his attorney, then at each one of us at the table and said, "I know who killed Gary Corso, his girlfriend, Leonard Capolla, and why."

Patrick Johns had our undivided attention. None of us expected that he'd have information about the murders. Johns lit another cigarette and waited for a reaction. Zack, like all of us, was hungry to solve the murders and asked bluntly, "Pat, what do want in exchange for this information?"

Johns stared back at Zack and said, "I want complete immunity."

Zack snapped back, "You would have to have firsthand knowledge of the killings, and be willing to testify in open court."

Johns turned to his lawyer and whispered something in his ear. Cullen, then said, "My client can put the killers behind bars."

Zack paused for a second and said, "Excuse me," and left the room. In less than thirty minutes he returned, with a written proffer for immunity, and said with authority, "I've conferred with the DA, your client will be granted immunity, if he has firsthand knowledge of the murders."

"Well then, we can proceed. Patrick, please sign the proffer under ADA Friedman's name. Please continue, Patrick."

"Me and Shorty Newcomb killed Gary and his girlfriend on the orders of Dante Malatesta. Shorty also killed Lenard Capolla on Dante's orders. Shorty lay in wait for Lenny. He unscrewed the light bulb in the vestibule of Lenny's building and shot him in the head when he walked into his house."

I interrupted, "How can we prove what you say?"

Without hesitation, Johns replied, "Dante told me to get rid of the guns, but I hid them under the floor boards in my sister's attic. Ballistics will confirm that the bullets that killed them came from those guns."

Nulligan shouted out, "Why did Malatesta order the killings?"

"I don't know." He replied. "You'll have to ask him. I just follow orders."

Zack continued with the questions. "Pat, where's the money and why'd you take it?"

Johns wrestled with Zack's question for a split second and said, "The pill I just took is for my heart. I'm dying of congestive heart failure. My doctor says maybe I'll live another year, if I'm lucky. The money is in a duffle bag in my sister's attic in South Salem, New York. I'd planned to give it to my son and my sister."

We were riveted by Johns' confession. He was a material witness in the money laundering case, and, more importantly, he was one of the shooters in the murder investigations. We'll house him in the Westchester County Jail for court proceedings. Zack Friedman anxiously began writing arrest warrants for Dante Malatesta, James Newcomb, and Dante's Uncle Dom. By now, Malatesta has probably figured out that we tapped his uncle's phone. We were hoping he wouldn't find the bugs, keep talking, and dig himself deeper into a hole. In any event we have to get to him before he disappears in the wind.

CHAPTER THIRTY

As luck would have it, just before we took Johns into custody, Malatesta was overheard on the bugs taking about the murders with his uncle. The day of reckoning was at hand. At 3:00 A.M. the next morning, Malatesta, his Uncle Dom, and James Shorty Newcomb were taken into custody. Malatesta, immediately called his lawyer, as did Newcomb. The detectives who arrested Shorty said that he became belligerent and resisted arrest. They were forced to taser him.

By 6:30 A.M., the defendants had been fingerprinted and photographed. They were scheduled to be arraigned before County Court Judge Robert Noury on charges of money laundering and murder. Before Dante's arraignment, we wanted a shot at flipping him, or in laymen's language, offering him a deal that he can't refuse. We knew that if he talks, he could give us Carmine Corso.

Dante, and his lawyer, Marty Goldstein were escorted into the interview room by two detectives. Friedman, Joe and I were already seated at the interview table. The damning tape of Dante discussing the murders was ready to be played. As soon as they were seated, Friedman turned on the recorder. Dante's eyes widened as he listened intently. In an instant, his demeanor changed. His head dropped and he slumped down in his seat. His hopeless glance at his attorney was revealing. He knew that he was looking at life in prison, possibly without parole. He turned to Goldstein and said, "Marty, how can I help myself?"

It's not often that a defense attorney is at a loss for words. He looked across the table at Zack and said, "Mr. Friedman, what are our options?"

Zack leaned forward; his eyes centered on Dante. "We want him to tell us about his involvement in the murders. We know from our surveillance that Mr. Malatesta reports to Carmine Corso. Most importantly, we want your client to testify about Corso's involvement in his laundering of monies from his illegal activities, and his knowledge of other crimes that Mr. Corso has committed. There are no promises, but his cooperation will certainly be brought to the attention of the court at sentencing. "

Goldstein, who's been representing mobsters for years, asked to speak with Malatesta privately. We left the room. Upon returning, Goldstein said that his client is willing to answer all questions, and testify about his involvement in the murders. He'll also willing to testify about his dealings with his Capo, Carmine Corso.

The first thing Zack said, "Dante, we insist you to answer truthfully. If not, all bets are off." Dante nodded in agreement. Zack continued, "I'd like Detective Santorsola to read you yours rights again, this time in the presence of your attorney. Then I'll proceed."

I read him his rights for the record.

"So let's begin. Dante, why did you order the murders of Gary Corso, Leonard Capolla, and Clare Iverson?"

Dante, coldly said, "Because I was ordered to."

Zack snapped back. "Because you were ordered to?"

"Yes, I was ordered to have them killed."

I couldn't help myself, I jumped in. "Ordered by who?"

Dante paused, took a breath, and said, "I was ordered by Gary's father Carmine, to kill em." What he just said shocked everyone in the room. I don't know about anyone else, but he sent chills up my spine.

We sat there in total silence, frozen in our seats, trying to comprehend what Malatesta just said. The thought of a father having his son murdered was unfathomable. Finally, Zack was able to force the question. "Why? Why would Carmine kill his own son?"

Malatesta coldly said, "I didn't understand why. I guess he's a psychopath but I'm a soldier. I follow orders. The only thing I can think of is that Gary and Lenny turned the business into a cash cow. He's a greedy son of a bitch, one hundred percent evil, and wanted the business back. When Gary and Lenny wouldn't sell it back, I guess Carmine had them killed. Like I said, the only thing Carmine cares about is money and power. I don't know why, but I could tell by the way Carmine spoke about Gary that he didn't care about him like a normal father should. I could never understand why Carmine resented his son. As far as Lenny goes, he owned half the business. He had Lenny killed so it would look like a Mafia turf war."

Nulligan, beside himself with anger snarled, "The fucking guy has no soul."

Dante replied with crushing certainty, "It was just business. Like I said, the psychopathic bastard had his own son killed, and ordered the hit on you, Santorsola. You were getting to close to Dana, and maybe too close to solving the murders. As I said, the bastard had his own flesh and blood slaughtered. Nobody meddles with Carmine's world. Nobody!"

I thought that I had seen and heard everything. I was wrong. I'd lost total faith in humanity. It's too bad that there's no death penalty in New York State, because Carmine deserves to fry.

CHAPTER THIRTY ONE

Two teams of detectives drove into C & C Waste Management. I was assigned to one of the teams. Garbage men were in their trucks, about to leave, when we skidded into the parking lot, creating a lot of dust. Carmine Corso was standing in the yard. He looked like his worst nightmare was about to unfold. He was right. In a complete panic, Corso bolted for the stairs. I was right on his heels. Before he reached the top of the stairs, I tackled him, and snapped handcuffs on him. "What's this all about Santorsola?"

I got up real close and personal. My lips almost rested against his ear. "Carmine, you piece of shit, you're under arrest for the murders of your son Gary, Leonard Capolla, and Clare Iverson!"

"Fuck you!" His head slumped down against the building as his breathing quickened. "I want to speak to my lawyer." Carmine remained silent as I led him down the stairs, and shoved him into the back of the police car.

Additional teams of detectives had been dispatched to arrest Jack Shaw, private investigator, and Mitch Humphrey, the AT&T employee. Spencer Johnstone was arrested later that afternoon in Fort Worth, by FBI agents. Captain Hugo Zapata-Feliz was arrested and detained by Mexican authorities, and will be brought back to the United States, and charged with international money laundering. There was a sigh of relief from everyone. The investigation was over. The only thing left was the successful prosecution of these low-lives.

The defendants had been arraigned on various charges and transported to the county jail awaiting their next court appearance. We ended up back in the squad room, popping bottles of champagne; celebrating the end of a very arduous homicide investigation. Even the DA was celebrating with us. He thanked us for our hard work and said that it was a two pronged celebration. Hogan raised his glass to the new chief. He was promoting Larry Christopher to permanent chief. We all toasted Larry, and then surrounded him, giving him high-fives, and pats on the back. Hogan thanked me for a great job and told me to take a few well deserved days off. The party continued until we ran out of champagne. We took the party to Jakes and continued celebrating until closing.

I didn't get home until 4:00 A.M. Denise had just moved back in last night. We were a couple again, and hopefully we'll remain a couple. She was asleep but heard me walk in. She jumped out of bed, wanting to hear about everything. When I told her that it was Gary's father that had him killed, she was horrified. She couldn't imagine a father having his own son murdered. We were so pumped that the case was finally put to rest, we stayed up for the rest of the night talking.

The next morning, the adrenalin was still pumping. I persuaded Denise to take the day off and spend the day with me. The murders had been solved and now I planned to put them behind me. We decided to have brunch at Tavern on the Green and then spend the rest of the day in Central Park. We arrived at the restaurant about noon, and were escorted to a table in the main dining room. In a matter of minutes, a waitress came over and placed menus in front of us. She didn't have to ask. I ordered a bottle of Veuve Clicquot champagne, and we both ordered Eggs Benedict Florentine. We relaxed there for an hour, enjoying our brunch, drinking champagne, and loving each others company.

We held hands as we walked out of the restaurant on 66th Street, crossed Fifth Avenue, and into Central Park. We slowly strolled through the park admiring the foliage, and watched people as they sailed their miniature sailboats on the lake. We were definitely caught up in the moment and every so often we'd stop and kiss. She said that I seemed to be much more relaxed and carefree. Of course I was. I was no longer slated for death. We walked around the lake and noticed a few more lovers, sitting on blankets, picnicking. Denise held my hand and told me how much she loved me and how happy she was. Pointing to the two story boathouse at the east end of the lake, Denise said, "Oh, Frankie. Let's take a boat ride."

"That sounds wonderful. Let's do it."

She tugged at my arm, dragging me to the boathouse. We rented a boat, and rowed lazily around the lake while she lay back on the seat soaking up the sun. The champagne we drank at brunch certainly put us in a tranquil mood. The first thing we did when we docked the rowboat was to buy two large ice cream cones from one of the vendors, and sat on a bench devouring them. Denise could tell that I was winding down after this extremely trying case. We were both able to see the light at the end of the tunnel. The bad guys were locked up and I could breathe in some fresh air. We decided that since we were in the city, we would have dinner at Connolly's Pub on East 47th Street, and then and spend the night at the Plaza Hotel. It was a perfect day; one of the best days of my life.

CHAPTER THIRTY TWO

Before I knew it, it was Monday morning and I was back in the office, breathing easy, now that Carmine Corso and the rest of the vermin were in jail, where they belong. I was sitting at my desk, drinking a cup of coffee, when out of the blue, Clare Iverson's mother called me. "What a surprise Mrs. Iverson." She thanked me for bringing her daughters killers to justice and said that she would like to thank me in person. I said that I'd be happy to meet with her.

Later that day, Mrs. Iverson arrived at the office. I escorted her to the conference room. She was a pretty woman, in her late fifties, elegantly dressed. Clutching her purse, she said, "Frank, thank you for seeing me. Mr. Hogan called me last week and told me that you were responsible for catching my daughter's killers. Thank you. Clare was a wonderful daughter. I have many cherished memories of her growing up. She always wanted to be a dancer."

"Mrs. Iverson, I'm so sorry for your loss. I can only imagine your sorrow."

She looked like was in a great deal of pain. She slowly unzipped her purse and took out what looked like a book, wrapped in brown paper, and handed it to me. Almost whispering, she said, "I discovered this yesterday. This will explain everything. I would like it back when you're done with it." She got up, as did I. She extended her hand and walked out.

Minutes after she left, I was called out on an emergency. Joe had locked his keys in his car, and he asked me to bring him a spare set. Before leaving, I locked the package in my desk. It wasn't until after 4:00 P.M. until I returned to the office. I brought back a cup of coffee, sat down, unlocking my desk drawer. I took out the package and opened it. It was a journal. On the inside cover, Clare Iverson's name was inscribed. I began to read her most intimate thoughts.

Most of the entries were mundane, *a new hairdresser…. a girl's night out…..a bachelorette party…. planning a surprise birthday party for a friend.* Then, whammy! Her January 1st entry. *My boyfriend has become obsessed with me..... My lover is very controlling.....He wants me always....all the time.... He wants to know who I call, and see, and how much time I spend with friends.....It's getting to be too much.... He has such a hold on me.....*

I took too much from him.....Now he's taking too much from me.

The trips, the jewels, the cars, and the money. His wife and family know nothing about our affair.... He says that he can not live without me.... I live a very luxurious lifestyle thanks to him, but I don't love him... Never did.... In the beginning it was fabulous....Nothing but good times....Not anymore..... I'm in over my head..... Last month, we had an argument..... He became so violent.... I was terrified....He raised his fist to hit me, but stopped himself at the last second....He promised he would never do that again....I don't believe him....I know all about his Mafia life.

I sat there, astounded. It was reading like a romance novel. I wanted to know more. The next entry shed even more light on Clare's story. *Last night my boyfriend arranged for me to attend a big charity event at the Waldorf Astoria in N.Y.C.... He was there with his wife and some family members. My job was to fawn over a new Mercedes Benz that was to be auctioned off that night..... I know that he just likes to keep an eye on me..... All of a sudden, I spotted a man that I couldn't take my eyes off of..... Our eyes locked.....We couldn't break the stare..... I longed to be near him.....I never had a feeling like this before. We connected and I gave him my number.*

My eye stopped on another riveting entry. *Gary called me the next day...I could feel my heart thumping, thumping..... The world drifted away..... Only the two of us existed.....There was no one else.....They say that love is indescribable.... It's true....When we met, I felt my life begin....Common sense goes out the window....There is only one place I will ever be happy, in Gary's arms....He's wild about me too.....How can life go topsy-turvy like this?... We are planning our future together.*

I thumbed through a few more pages and stopped at her next entry that mentioned Gary. *He can't know about Gary and me....We are extremely careful....We both know what could happen if we are found out.... Gary and I are bound together by love....We have no other choice..... We will be together.... I love him...he loves me.... I only wish it were that simple.*

The very next page set me back on my heels. It freaking blew my mind. Clare wrote: *I discovered all too quickly that my 3-year affair with Carmine was doomed. My true love is Gary, Carmines son....I had to confess the details of my affair with Carmine to Gary....How could this happen.....The one forbidden factor...The inevitable fact....We were in a dangerous love triangle. Our feelings were so strong.... Gary will let nothing stand in our way. We will be together despite Carmine.*

Clare went on to write.....*I just took a home pregnancy test...It was positive...I'm pregnant!!! I called Gary right away...He was overcome with happiness....If it's a boy, our son will be named Gary.... Gary is going to confront his father, and tell him about us..... I'm frightened about what Carmine might do!*

This is unbelievable, a stunning revelation. I can hardly believe what I'm reading. Carmine, Clare, Gary, it was a reckless love triangle. Now it all makes sense.

Clare had every word underlined on her next entry: <u>*Gary confronted his father last night... He told Carmine that we are in love and I was going to have his baby.... Carmine went berserk.....He attacked Gary with a hammer...There was a fight....Gary fought him off...Gary's arm was injured....Carmine told Gary that I belonged to him...and that Gary will not have me...Carmine said he can not live without me....How could we do this to him...We would be sorry we were ever born...Carmine's going to make both our lives a living hell....Gary told Carmine that we are going to start a new life together....He was divorcing Dana...His father's threats didn't matter....For the first time, Gary saw the evil and jealousy in his father's eyes.*</u>

It was clear to me. Carmine didn't kill his son over the business. He had him killed because he was blindly jealous of Gary and Clare.

Clare's last entry in her journal: *My heart stopped again today.... I thought I saw one of Carmine's goons following me..... I'm meeting Gary tonight....We're planning on getting away.... I'm gonna tell my mom tomorrow....I hope and pray that things will work out for Gary, me and the baby.*

I put the journal down, trying to comprehend the whole sordid affair, but for the life of me, I couldn't bring myself to understand it. If Clare's mother hadn't found this journal, Clare would have taken this story to her grave. Now, the world will know the true intent behind "The Garbage Murders." They had absolutely nothing to do with the private sanitation industry. Carmine couldn't control his jealousy. That green eyed monster put an end to many lives.

I picked up the phone and called Hogan's office. "Mr. Hogan, I'd like to meet with you as soon as possible. Something's come up. I just got a message from Heaven."

EPILOUGE

Since our money laundering case had its tentacles reaching into Mexico, Westchester County District Attorney John Hogan turned the case over to the United States Attorneys Office, Southern District of New York. As it turned out, Patrick Johns was a star witness in both the state homicide trials and the federal money laundering trial. In each jurisdiction the prosecutor decided to try each individual separately. Shortly after the trials, Patrick Johns passed away from congestive heart failure.

Hugo-Zapata-Feliz decided not to go to trial and pleaded guilty to international money laundering. He was sentenced to 10-20 years in Federal Prison. He is serving his time in Beaumont, Texas.

Spencer Johnstone was also convicted of international money laundering and sentenced to 10-20 years. He's serving his time in Federal Prison, in Bastrop, Texas.

Dante Malatesta testified in State Court. His testimony led to the conviction of Carmine Corso for ordering the murders. For his cooperation, Malatesta received a sentence of five years in Sing Sing Correctional Facility and will be placed into witness protection upon his release. His Uncle Dominick was convicted of conspiracy to commit murder and sentenced to 15-20 years. He's serving his time in Coxsackie Correctional Facility in upstate NY.

Jack Shaw was convicted of commercial bribery of a telephone company employee and conspiracy to commit murder. He had his private investigators license revoked. He was sentenced to 10-20 years in Coxsackie Correctional Facility, where he is not eligible for parole until 2018.

Mitch Humphrey, the AT & T security employee, was convicted of Grand Larceny of telephone company records and sentenced to five years' probation. He was fired by the telephone company.

James "Shorty" Newcomb was convicted at trial and sentenced to 25 years to life for the murders of Leonard Capolla, Gary Corso and Clare Iverson.

He is currently serving his time in the Clinton Correctional Facility in Dannemore, NY. He's not eligible for parole until 2030.

Carmine Corso refused to utter a word at his trial. He was sentenced to 25 years to life, without the possibility of parole. His daughter-in- law Dana Corso looked on loathsomely as he was lead out of the courtroom in handcuffs. He is serving his time, in Attica Correctional Facility in Attica, NY.

We never could prove that Carmine Corso ordered the murders of Anton Cermack and Gennaro Balistrieri. I suspect that Carmine had them killed because he was afraid that they might cooperate if arrested.

Well, as for me, Frank Santorsola A/K/A Frank Miranda, my guess is that I'll be assigned to another intriguing case. In the meantime, John Hogan has invited me several times to play golf with him at the Westchester Country Club. At the moment, LaVita Bella!

The End

For sales, speaking opportunities for Mr. Santorsola, or other inquiries, please contact us at:

Baxter Productions Inc.
308 Main St
New Rochelle NY 10801
(914) 576-8706
pressoffice@baxterproductionsmedia.com

41608718R00126

Made in the USA
Middletown, DE
18 March 2017